MANAGEMENT TRAINING FOR REAL

Management Training For Real

Hawdon Hague
Managing Partner of Context Training

Institute of Personnel Management
5 Winsley Street, Oxford Circus, London W1N 7AQ

First published May 1973

© 1973 Hawdon Hague

No part of this publication
may be reproduced in any
form without written permission

ISBN 0 85292 0 83 0

Set in 10*pt Garamond*
Printed in Great Britain
by T. & W. Goulding Ltd.
Bristol & London

Contents

Appendices

Figures

Introduction

The extent to which management training is carried out in the hypothetical is not generally realized. Courses are necessarily general and somewhat abstract; case studies, by definition, apply somewhere else and even role playing, no matter how realistic, can be done by people who will say 'but it doesn't apply to me'. Off the job training is relatively new for operatives, but it has always been taken for granted that managers would be trained off the job: that that was the only way to do it.

On the job management training is not only possible, it is a more powerful tool. A man's job is his most powerful (work) influence, together with the help or reaction he gets from his boss. Changing his job, or coaching him in it, are therefore important ways to train him, whether the planning and coaching is done by a line superior or a specialist.

Other ways of using the real situation as a training vehicle are to set up projects: projects within the organization and dealing with actual problems. They can be individual or group problems, and look at one function or several, but there is nothing hypothetical about them and their relevance and importance are undeniable. The learning impact is greater and, when a lesson is taken, the taker cannot say it doesn't apply to him.

Little attention has been paid until recently to setting management training in a real context and the idea of trainers without classrooms and syndicate rooms seems almost bizarre. In the new approach, the trainer makes learning capital out of whatever turns up, or so structures the actual situation that maximum learning takes place. In either case, it is the situation that provides the opportunity and the stimulus for the manager to develop himself— which is the key to the learning impact. The trainer's role is a very different one, the line superior is an important part of the process and every manager has the major responsibility for developing himself.

Training in a real context is much more likely to change the way a manager manages, which is the reason for writing this book. However, almost all assumptions and preconceptions about management training have to be changed and the text will therefore go on to spell out what to do and why, the dangers to avoid and also what reorientation is necessary.

Section I

What to do and why

1 Why train in the real situation?

Management training in the real situation is far from easy and presents a degree of difficulty not experienced in more traditional forms of training. One section of this book will discuss the difficulties. The ways to overcome them are never completely successful, so the question arises: why should you embark on such a stormy voyage? Why not write off management training as a failure? The case for training in the real situation can be summed up by saying that it offers the chance of greater effectiveness. Where training has so far been ineffective, this can to a large extent be explained and many of the factors in the explanation provide the justification for the new approach to management training.

Learning theory

It is not necessary to go into any of the more abstruse learning theories to list certain basic principles which influence adult learning. One of the best definitions of learning is 'the modification of behaviour through experience' and it will strike you that a teacher may not be necessary. When you think of it, most learning is self-learning, certainly with adults. If our concern is to teach, or to persuade a manager to modify his behaviour in certain directions, we must therefore construct a situation in which he has suitable experiences and where he will, it is hoped, draw suitable conclusions from them.

This definition is not inappropriate even in junior schools, where most of the original work in learning theory has been carried out. We think of children learning from their teachers and their books, but learning by discovery is increasingly employed and teachers design learning situations instead of trying to put across all the knowledge themselves. It follows that the teacher cannot prescribe precisely what lessons are taken, or in what order. But the child is stimulated to ask questions or to find out for himself, and will the better remember what he discovers. For example, a class visit to an old castle on a rock might trigger off questions on history, rock formation or mathematical ideas on how to measure its height: every child is likely to react in a questioning and learning way.

If teaching by formal lecturing methods is not the best method with young children, whose minds are alert and who are keen to learn, it is unlikely to be successful with managers of 30 plus, who have a measure of success behind them and the basic assumption that they know all they need to know, with the possible exception of some new or refined techniques. Assuming that we want managers to 'learn' in rather wider areas than this, it follows that they will respond only to experiences and by drawing their own conclusions from them. A management teacher should therefore design learning situations. He can try to ensure that the manager reflects on his own experiences and can sometimes suggest the lessons to be drawn; but the focus is on learning, rather than teaching and this basic point has so far been ignored.

There are many other reasons why formal teaching methods are ineffective in getting experienced managers, as opposed to trainees in their early 20s, to modify their behaviour. An experienced manager has difficulty in learning from formal teaching because:

i   he is not good at abstracting from a general lecture what is relevant to his own situation

ii he will remember very little at the end of an hour's lecture, and next to nothing three weeks later if he has not done anything with the ideas put across

iii there are problems in implementing the new ideas, even if the lessons are taken. His organization may not allow him to do so (the 're-entry' problem), there may not be opportunities, things turn out rather differently from the way envisaged in the lecture, minor complications arise and the experiment gradually fizzles out.

It is a painful experience for a lecturer to test how much has been distilled and remembered from his lecture. The figure of 20 per cent, is usual and he cannot improve on it by saying the important parts twice and including them in a hand-out note. The mind has to do something fairly quickly with a new fact or idea if it is to be remembered: this is known technically as 'reinforcement'. Lectures would be suitable vehicles for learning if students took short notes during a lecture, wrote them up fully in the evening, put the new ideas in a report at the end of the course and implemented them within a week. Such reinforcement is rare and most of what is heard is quickly forgotten.

Case studies are better in that new ideas and concepts are being used but the question of abstracting what is relevant to one's own job remains, and this 'transfer' is not easy. Many adults do not abstract well and we all have a defence mechanism which assures us that whatever principle is being propounded, and no matter how logical it seems, it does not apply to us. This is rationalized in various ways: either it is all right for big firms or for a manufacturing concern but doesn't apply to ours, or we are so big we've got a special department to look after that, or it's exactly what our boss ought to do. To make a manager learn, the complacency barrier must be overcome: this 'unfreezing' is difficult if not impossible in a classroom where, by convention, you mustn't risk upsetting the student.

If managers are to learn by discovery, it follows they must take the initiative in their self-development. Schoolchildren have a thirst for knowledge but this motivation is far from automatic with experienced managers: some genuinely have minds which are continually questioning and self-critical but the majority fall into routine ways of thinking and translate all experiences into confirmation of established views and practices. The same majority approach learning with something akin to fear: it is hard work and—in a classroom form —demeaning, while it might show up inadequacies or threaten the self-image. Adults therefore need a strong incentive to start a learning process. This can take the form of knowing that promotion prospects would be improved by success or the new idea may be seen as directly relevant and helpful to the immediate job. Once a manager has seen that something can actually help him, he will need no further external motivation. It is gratifying to know that he can still learn new tricks. The problem is getting to this stage, and it is more likely to result from an exercise in a real situation than in a hypothetical one.

Individuality of needs

The other main reason why the course approach to management training is ineffective is that managers' needs are individual to themselves, whereas a course must be generalized. In particular many needs stem from the manager's perception of himself, and of his role within the organization, so that they border on psychological questions rather than management techniques.

Talking of manager's development needs in this way automatically widens the discussion from the normal training needs analysis which, being somewhat mechanistic in approach, produces mechanistic needs (such as courses). Development needs should be considered as those factors which limit a manager's effectiveness; these, it will be widely agreed, are more bound up with attitudes or personality than with, say, network analysis and discounted cash flow. Personality can be changed only to a limited extent and attitudes cannot be changed in much under a year, but, if this is where the greatest improvement is available, the attempt must be made. Robert Townsend[1] has said that managers use less than 25 per cent of their intellect at work and, if we are thinking about the creative or entrepreneurial side of intellect, few would disagree.

[1] TOWNSEND, R. Address to the Industrial Society, July 1971.

Those managers in their 30s or later who work assiduously enough from 9 am to 5 pm, but follow established routines rather than look for anything new, are perhaps the greatest challenge to management education. Some may never have had any particular ambition but the rest have switched off, for one reason or another. The cruel but all too apt phrase, the male menopause, describes a state when a man realizes that he is not going to rise much further, if at all, and that the certainty and severity of penalty if he sticks his neck out and loses are both greater than the chance of reward if he wins. When there is little advancement to be hoped for, the attention turns to avoiding demotion. This circumstance, which can hit a man at 35, when he still has 30 years to work, can be allied with the Peter Principle[1] whereby people are promoted to one level beyond their competence, and substitute 'busy' tasks for those they should be doing. Add Rosemary Stewart's picture[2] of the man who is 'busy' because it meets his ego needs and we can understand the familiar picture of managers bustling about while nothing ever improves.

The Mant Report[3] provides the best known statement that individual managers have individual needs and that these are tied up with attitudes, if not mental blocks. It deserves further study because little is now remembered about it except that it discussed in-company training and listed seven caricatures of managment types: for example, the Mobile manager who changes jobs when necessary to his own progress, the Thwarted manager whose ability has been submerged by frustration, the Old Boy manager who uses his considerable talents to make life cushy for himself and the Backbone manager with little intelligence and little else to be said in his favour except that he, almost alone, gets the work out. But there was much more to the report. The diverse needs of the different types were spelled out: courses would terrify the

[1] PETER, L. J. and HULL, R. The Peter Principle, Souvenir Press, 1969.
[2] STEWART, R. Managers and their Jobs, Macmillan, 1967.
[3] MANT, A. The Experienced Manager, British Institute of Management, 1969.

17

Backbone manager but he needs to be kept mentally alert; the Old Boy needs a jolt he will resent at the time (but he would be glad he had been made to acquire some more saleable skills if he was made redundant at 48); even the man who is likely to leave can be induced to make a considerable contribution and would be the more likely to stay.

The caricatures were not meant to be exhaustive but they show the variety of experienced manager learning needs and also the extent to which they derive from the individual's situation in the company and from his perception of it. The limiting factors on an experienced manager's intellectual contribution are likely to be emotional, part illogical, and very much tied up with the restriction he feels his boss or the organization impose upon him. Most managers feel that their ability to do their best is circumscribed in some way and, whether their feeling is correct or not, this limits their endeavour. It follows that these needs can be dealt with only in the actual situation and must start with the manager's perception of it. It could be either the perception or the situation that needs to be changed, but in either case this is a far cry from instruction in management techniques or human relations. Until blocks to motivation are removed, the subjects covered in normal courses are peripheral and probably futile. The basic needs are individual and job-centred; they lie in areas of psychology/personality/prejudice that we normally prefer not to talk about. One can only develop managers if one is aware of these factors and tackles them at source.

2 Planned experience

There is nothing new in planned experience or, rather, there is nothing new in the concept. Job rotations have for long figured at the top of every list of management development tools—although they have probably been much less common in practice. Shorter job assignments have long been known, especially for graduate trainees and junior management, also planned experience at trainee level, which often included a six month or longer period when the trainee just observed several departments. This last practice (the Cook's Tour) produced more frustration than learning. The Cook's Tour broke the principle of learning by doing. The other planned experiences have been talked about for a long time but should be done more often and more deliberately. It is by experience that adults learn.

Job rotation

Job rotation has been sufficiently written about and is the procedure by which a manager changes his job, not as a promotion but to give him experience of more functions. Ideally, if a man is put in charge of several functions, he should have had direct experience of all of them.

There are two theoretical problems: (i) the ideal length of time to hold each job, striking the happy balance between staying so long that the manager ceases to be stimulated by it rotating him so quickly that he gains only superficial impressions and has moved on to his next job before his mistakes catch up with him; (ii) the extent to which managers can change functions or products. If one believes that management is a professional skill that can be applied anywhere, and that technical knowledge becomes progressively less important as one rises in the hierarchy, there is a case for quite dramatic job rotations for anyone who might become a managing director or divisional chief executive. And yet this is just where the eminently sensible theory is least put into practice. How many newly promoted chief executives have an adequate appreciation of all the functions they then control? Most have been promoted because of their success in one function, and may have a smattering of a second, but nearly all have major gaps in their knowledge. This leads to the natural temptation to over-supervise one's old function and never to get to unbiased grips with the others. (The correct course would be to spend most time in the strange functions but that would require unusual fairmindedness and also some crisis-free months.) The failure to produce properly qualified general managers is one of the more serious indictments of management development to date.

To enquire why the most obvious steps in career planning are not taken is to reveal many of the causes of the in-effectiveness of management development. There is not enough spare managerial capacity at the higher levels to allow this sort of rotation, and career planning is done, if at all, by someone junior to the functional directors. What job rotations do take place are generally at lower levels, usually within the same overall function. This is sensible where technical knowledge is vital; small exchanges may provide sufficient stretching for those of limited ability. Rotation of middle-aged middle managers is comparatively rare, and this is another area where it would seem obviously desirable. How better to stop managers getting into a rut than to change their jobs from time to time, or at least give them some new responsibilities while taking some others away? The reason why backbone managers are not rotated is that it is easiest to leave them where they are; they would probably complain if moved from their familiar job and work group. Yet the armed services achieve job rotation without anyone feeling aggrieved because everyone is moved at least every three years, quite often into a different function.

Whether you rotate backbone managers during the last 30 years of their working life depends on your values: life will be easier and short term profits will be greater if you don't, managers will stay mentally alert for longer if you do, and your long term managerial assets will be greater. The length of time in one job also depends on company values. From the point of view of the manager's learning, he has probably extracted most of the value from a job within two years: from an output point of view, he will contribute most if left much longer. The reason lip service is paid to job rotation could be that the implied value system is a demanding one, viz:

that managers make up a major asset whose long term growth is as important as current profits

that sufficient reserves of managerial talent be carried to allow the timing of rotations to be planned and not dictated by emergencies

the length of time a manager stays in a job should be dictated by how much he is learning from it rather than how much he is contributing in it

it is important to keep managers mentally alert and thinking about the way they are doing their jobs, although this runs counter to the natural inertias and will produce shrieks of pain

losing a manager because you failed to prod him into life is preferable to 25 years of gradually diminishing performance because you don't even make the attempt

that management development is as important as any other function and should be represented accordingly.

Job rotation is the most obvious tool in the armoury of management learning in the real situation. All managers should therefore have some significant change of responsibilities at intervals of between one and three years. The rotation should mean being sent to completely new functions as high flyers get near to the top; it should be partial for first line managers, where technical competence is paramount, or for limited middle managers. The effectiveness of career planning can in fact be measured by:

the percentage of new appointments where the choice and timing was in accordance with the appointee's career plan

the proportion of general management appointments where the appointee has sufficient breadth of experience

the number of times external recruitment is needed

the number of managers who have had no job change in three years.

Short term programmes

A short term programme is either a short term rotation or else a period of observation. The former can be an effective learning experience when relatively close jobs are interchanged at lower level. For example, production manager and production controller can exchange jobs for six months and then return to their former roles. Either is still available if required for a particularly knotty query on his old job and each gets a considerable insight into his own job by seeing it from next door. Crucial factors in this operation are the fact that the rotation is not too drastic and the men revert to their original jobs (otherwise the six month exercise would be too superficial). This is a simple way of bringing about increased understanding and learning. It takes little organizing and no teaching, and is enjoyable as well as instructive. It is learning in a very acceptable form.

3 Coaching by superior

There is no doubt that the best method of management teaching, in the real situation or anywhere else, is good coaching by one's boss. Research by General Electric showed that 300 managers said that their main developmental experience had been 'working for so and so', and many good UK managers attribute their strength to training given by a boss during their formative years. The techniques of coaching should therefore be studied by line manager and training specialist alike. If all managers made a reasonable attempt to coach their subordinates, there would be no need of management trainers; but unwillingness to coach is so widespread that the specialist will survive for some time yet. The techniques of coaching, as outlined below, are not particularly difficult, apart from keeping certain psychological considerations in mind, so we will also examine why this most powerful training tool is so little used. The reasons range from the pressures of short term results to the inadequacy and emotional insecurity of senior managers, and firms must get their organization and staffing broadly right before coaching can take place. One of the themes of this book is that correct teaching is part and parcel of correct management and not something to be sneaked in by specialists when bad management is not looking: this is particularly true with coaching.

Appraisals

Appraisal interviews are the most formalized coaching

situation. A recent IPM publication[1] has covered the subject fully: I do not want to go into the arguments for and against such interviews except to say that, if coaching was taking place regularly, the annual interview would lose its particular significance—and its particular traumas. Also, the coaching aspect needs to be highlighted, because it can provide further justification for a potentially embarrassing meeting that is still widely ducked. (The statement by McGregor[2] that 'Managers do not like to play God' is often given as the reason why appraisers are reluctant, but I suspect that the reluctance stems more from the fear of being exposed as an arbitrary deity than dislike of the power itself).

Management by objectives (MBO) has made a valuable contribution by focusing attention on the achievement of objectives and by removing discussion of personality characteristics from the appraisal. On the other hand, by focusing on ends rather than means it has played down the coaching possibilities of the situation. If a superior says: 'You should have produced a 100 tons a week, but you achieved only 80 tons: what are you going to do about it?', he is being objective and encouraging the subordinate to make his own decisions but much of the coaching opportunity is lost. To coach, the superior must go into the How of the desired improvement and not just ask for shortfalls to be explained. A walk-out may be the explanation for a shortfall, but the manager needs to know whether it was thought to be his fault and if it was due to something he could improve. If so, is it a question of learning a technique, practising a new style or virtually changing personality? The superior need not give his own direct answers to these questions but he must ensure that the subordinate faces them, and he must not shrink from subjective comment if the subordinate, for example, cannot see how to improve.

The over-riding consideration in appraisals is the spirit

[1] RANDELL, G et al. Staff Appraisal, Institute of Personnel Management (IPM), 1972.
[2] McGREGOR, D. An Uneasy Look at Performance Appraisal, Harvard Business Review, May/June 1967.

of the interview. The subordinate's potential resentment will disappear if the superior accepts responsibility for any weaknesses, and if they jointly make plans to overcome them. If the subordinate feels that the concern is genuine, that the aim is to help and not just to damn him and if hard plans are made, the appraisal interview becomes a coaching opportunity. Teaching at an annual interview would be ludicrous if not supplemented by other coaching, but, if the annual meeting is held, the coaching aspect should be given prominence in reviewing learning, analysing successes and stimulating and planning further development.

Other methods

First, what coaching is not: it is not going from time to time to see what a subordinate is doing and advising how to do it better; neither is it the fatherly passing on of hard-gained experience or telling a subordinate what to do, throwing in a short lecture for good measure. It is, rather, a question of making the subordinate aware of how he is managing, of controlled delegation and of using whatever situations arise as teaching opportunities. Coaching means establishing the right atmosphere of openness and partnership in planning and reviewing results.

Interfering in what a manager is doing is not coaching; setting up a slightly different situation or making him see the existing one from a different viewpoint is. Getting a manager to analyse his methods of operating, discussing alternatives and, when a major decision has been taken, reviewing the how as opposed to the what, is coaching. The aim is to make the pupil think and find out things for himself; discussions before and immediately after significant events will achieve that, as will the knowledge that he is being intelligently observed. You may prompt the pupil into asking for advice; if the request is genuine, ie neither flattery or abdication, this is good, but if possible content yourself with spelling out possibilities and leaving him with that most powerful of development tools—making a decision.

Much of the art of coaching is akin to that of delegation

and may well entail watching a subordinate make mistakes without interfering. There are times when the mistake would be so serious that you must intervene but it should be the rule not to prohibit, and not to specify the alternative course of action. You should ask questions to elicit whether your subordinate has thought through what he is doing, and whether he has considered the alternatives and the implications. If he had overlooked the latter, the questioning in itself might lead to a change of plan; if he had made a careful plan, but a bad one in your eyes, let him carry it out because you will then be well placed to conduct a review afterwards. You will be well informed and able to be quite gentle because many of the lessons will have been spotted by the trainee.

You can control the rate at which your subordinate takes on responsibilities, which is another aspect of delegation. Duties can thus be delegated one by one, instead of together on a sink or swim basis, and each new area can be properly talked through. To help structure this, list the decisions that may confront your subordinate and classify them as follows:

1 do as you think fit
2 do as you think fit but tell me afterwards for information
3 ask me before you take any decision

Category 2 is for areas where you ought to be informed so that you do not look silly if somebody else refers to the matter, but it is an important—and little used—classification for development purposes. There ought to be a steady progression from category 3 to category 2 if you are coaching and delegating correctly; if you repeat the classification at six-monthly intervals, you can even measure your success in extending his responsibilities.

Those managers who attribute their strength to the attention of one of their early bosses say that the profitable time was spent, not in discussing their own jobs, but in looking at higher level problems. A good coach will take his subordinate to meetings, under the pretext of minute-taking, for example, but really for his interest. Discussion beforehand of tactics, the politics involved and why the meeting was called, plus review later of what was unexpected are interesting and instructive to the trainee, who is in no way on the defensive and may be flattered at being shown the difficulties of his seniors. It is often claimed that political in-fighting is a necessary skill and this is probably the only way it can be taught. Similarly, someone who has seen his boss carry the day at a meeting because he alone had prepared for it will take the importance of preparation to heart.

Setting a special project is a method which overlaps with the content of chapter 5, but is nonetheless an important coaching tool and ensures that the trainee does not spend all his time on the routine aspects of his job. Other tools are:

1 responsibility during your holidays. Announce, like Robert Townsend,[1] that you will support his decisions on your return. That way you will get decisions and development, not just a pile of acknowledged letters in your pending tray and some infuriated customers

2 representing you at meetings; again with power to act; discuss what he did: that is good coaching

3 membership of professional or other societies; encourage him to take an active part

4 getting him to set projects for his own subordinates and possibly sitting in yourself on the review sessions

5 giving him a book to read or sending him on a course, and setting a specific task to do with what he learns (eg writing a report on how it would apply to . . . .).

This form of coaching is time-consuming because the junior is being included in meetings he would not otherwise have gone to, and the superior is spending time discussing his own problems, mainly for the benefit of the junior. It also follows that the tools of the coach are not punishment for mistakes, or any reward for success other than the feeling of being a bigger and better manager. This

[1] TOWNSEND, R. *Up the Organisation*, Michael Joseph, 1970.

atmosphere cannot be created unless the organization as a whole is committed to developing its people, but establishing the right atmosphere for coaching is more important than any of the individual tools.

Rules for coaching

A Recognition of opportunity

Most situations provide coaching opportunities but anything new, unexpected or particularly significant is valuable. An unusual event in the subordinate's job always presents an opportunity because his normal performance is not in question and he will regard it as a challenge anyway. Also, situations do occur where the subordinate is making mistakes, but it is feasible to let him learn from them rather than overrule him. When an experience is recent, its learning impact is greatest, so you should be ready to coach at any time and make teaching capital out of whatever turns up.

There are two pre-requisites. One is a plan of the general areas and direction in which you want to develop your subordinate, which may or may not have come out of performance appraisals; the other is a feel for when he is open to suggestions and when not. A shattering failure makes most people defensive at first, but possibly very open to suggestion a couple of days later. A success might lead to the automatic rejection of immediate criticism, so the coach should seek only to analyse the reasons for success and to discuss other applications of the same methods. A request for advice may or may not be a straightforward coaching opportunity, but it offers the chance to give good counsel or a good shake as appropriate.

Events or problems within your own job that you might bring your subordinate into fall into cases where you would genuinely welcome suggestions or where you are fairly confident that what you are doing is right. (If many of your decisions don't fall into either category, you've got problems, and you ought to see about getting some coaching!) You cannot spend all your time showing your subordinates your difficulties, but more of your time in contact with them should be devoted to developing them than to giving orders or passively 'supervising'. Coaching is a matter for daily contact and it should be part of everyday management.

B Beware of the defence mechanisms

The greatest barriers to learning are those we all erect to preserve our images of ourselves, and which come into operation most noticeably when we are criticized. Even the most intelligent and seemingly balanced man will say silly things when he feels himself attacked, and be quite unaware of it, although it is obvious to an observer what is happening. People react in different ways to criticism, but usually in ways which close their mind against suggestion: no learning will take place until, at least in their own eyes, they have justified themselves.

There are varieties of these defence mechanisms, and also a range of self-images. For example, some think of themselves as dynamic men of action, others as profoundly reasonable and unaffected by anything emotional, or as original thinkers or professional protesters. Criticism which threatens a man's self-image is rejected totally, if not violently, while other criticism which would cut somebody else to the quick might be relatively easy to accept. For example, a man of action would not resent criticism that he did not see all the alternatives and a man of vision would not mind being accused of ignoring details.

Some understanding of self-images and defence mechanisms is needed by any coach because they explain the most important rules. Direct criticism must usually be avoided unless it is in a less sensitive area for the particular recipient. An escape route for the self-esteem must always be provided. Equally, congratulations or suggestions must bolster the self-image and emphasize the factors which are important to the student. The response will be greatest if the learner feels that he might actually increase his value in his own eyes and in the eyes of those whose approval he seeks. You are trying to get him to develop himself and so you must appeal to his criteria, which may not be the same as your own.

The dangers are even more fundamental. Being asked to learn at all may threaten to force a man out of the comfortable position in which his self-image is fed and maintained; for example, the manager by flair and snap-decision might throw out the whole idea of training. All people, at all levels, are particularly sensitive on some issues; any attempts at coaching must be carefully approached and timed if they are not to trigger off a defensive reaction which would be non-productive. Adults resist, and probably even fear, the process of learning; the first one or two steps should be small and non-threatening and designed to lead almost certainly to success. After that, much more is possible.

C Do not attempt too much

If the subordinate has 16 faults, you will not change them all at once. If you mention more than three, he will switch off; if you want to tackle a fourth or fifth area, you will therefore have to keep your designs to yourself (which would not be impossible if, for example, you set a project). In selecting weaknesses to work on, choose either one or two where the present performance is unacceptable or where speedy improvement might be possible. Another strategy is to concentrate on two or three key result areas whose importance is such that they will be readily appreciated by the pupil and will form a natural subject for joint planning sessions. Success in key result areas has a marked effect on results and consequently on morale and further acceptance of coaching.

Most appraisal schemes and development plans have tended to concentrate on faults but it is often surprisingly possible to coach a man to make better use of his strengths. You may be able to alter his job slightly and give him more to do of the things he does well; the response may be so much greater that it is worth putting up with his weaknesses. Also, if you concentrate on his strengths, it will help your own morale and enable you to keep a more balanced view of him than if you spend time rehearsing the list of his irritating weaknesses.

Why coaching rarely happens

If coaching your subordinates is relatively easy, and by far the most effective form of training, why does it take place so infrequently? Some of the answers have been hinted at already: the embarrassment commonly caused by appraisal interviews, the difficulty of raising delicate issues, the volatile reactions to criticism. These are difficulties that can be overcome and they do not explain why coaching responsibilities are ducked.

The underlying fact is that few managers to date have wanted to coach. The most charitable explanation is the pressure of short term profit figures. Coaching is time-consuming, the benefits do not show up in the short term and may never be credited to the coach anyway. The feeling that the development of managers cannot justify 5-10 hours a week is therefore likely to be held on a company-wide basis: it is common in old fashioned, entrepreneurial firms and in the most sophisticated and budget-ridden. Organizational priorities prevail and it would be a brave Samaritan who stood out against the prevailing ethic. Equally, you cannot attempt to coach in an organization where jobs are insecure. In the right organization, you are promoted as soon as you have developed your successor but what if you are in the wrong organization? Again, if you are to tolerate some mistakes as conducive to learning, you must be in a company which permits this.

There are less charitable explanations for the absence of coaching, eg inadequacy. It does not occur to many managers to coach their subordinates, partly because they have never seen it done, but also because their subordinates might prove to be the more worthy. No one will let a subordinate in on his problems if he is floundering or cannot analyse what he is doing, or if he feels, even subconsciously, that only his rank and access to information give him authority over the subordinate. It requires high emotional security to want to coach: such security and maturity are rare because of factors such as bad promotions in the past, changes in markets and technologies and increases in executive stress.

Put at its blackest, coaching will often not take place without a change of organizational priorities, the removal of some managers and the promotion of more capable ones. But, once an organization has its values and staffing broadly right, coaching can become a normal and powerful tool for releasing managerial intelligence and initiative.

4 Coaching by third party

Coaching is a word much in vogue at present and somehow 'coaches' are more acceptable than 'trainers'. They are known to have rowed well themselves and they are better placed to comment on the teamwork. The metaphor is worth taking further because there is no question that it is the eight who will do the rowing, but no crew would dream of operating without a coach. The same is true of swimmers and singers who receive worldwide acclaim but do not feel this puts them beyond help by a coach. This sort of relationship, and humility, would be useful to managers.

Individual coaching (top management)

There are two types of individual coaching. One consists of short bursts of one-to-one tuition, the other is a longer exercise of at least three days which the coach spends continuously with the manager. The latter method is expensive and applicable to very senior managers; the shorter bursts can be applied more widely. Depth observation of senior managers is closest to the analogy of the swimming coach. Any senior man who has no superior in close contact is in a situation where he receives little or no personal criticism and he may well become dogmatic, capricious and out of touch. He may get conceited about his successes and blame his failures on external circumstances but, worst of all, he will cease to be self-critical and to learn from his experiences. There are many men in this position but some are now countering the danger by using an external coach (see Appendix IV).

There are some subjects which lend themselves especially well to individual coaching and indeed cannot properly be handled any other way, eg the use of time, delegation and decision-making. It is easy to think you are delegating to the hilt, and to deceive a casual caller but, if someone spends three days continuously with you, you realize you have spent time on tasks somebody else should have done and that people stopped you with trivial question. Fragmented and badly planned time is apparent to both parties, as is an irrational attitude to decisions, but only an observer who has spent long enough for the period not to be dismissed as untypical is in a position to raise such delicate issues.

The coach is faced with two possibilities: one is to ask questions fairly frequently such as 'Why did you do that?'; 'Why did you do it then?'; the other is to wait to the end of the day and ask the manager to begin the analysis. In either case, questioning must be the right approach rather than anything didactic because the coach is not in a position to say 'You should have. . . .' as he cannot know all the background. By asking questions like: 'What else could you have done? Did you consider such and such?' he makes the same points and prompts the manager into thinking about alternatives while giving him the chance to excuse himself by telling the coach of the many special circumstances of which he was unaware.

Unless the tutor has a specialist training, say in one of the decision techniques, he should concentrate on why things were done at a certain time, what was left undone that might have been done, what alternatives have been considered and whether sufficient alternatives had been generated. This might seem like a basic exercise in egg-sucking but the most basic management considerations are often the weakest. Another approach is to ask the manager to talk about his objectives and priorities. He may well have these set out in a formalized document, but it will probably help him to think through them or behind them and to discuss their implications with someone who has seen him trying to apply them. A questioning technique rather like that of the

34

supplementary question in the House of Commons is appropriate: the initial response is a reflex action but a clever follow-up question finds the reality, or the vagueness, behind the official reply.

The coach will rapidly see the areas that need attention. Lack of delegation or the number of trivial interruptions is easily spotted, as is whether or not there is a basic plan for the day and whether it is too easily blown off course. (If the manager has no interruptions, he is either supremely well-delegated or redundant, and it should be relatively simple to tell which.) Similarly the 'busy-ness', which means he likes to have a lot of people coming in and out, is readily apparent as is the type of decisiveness that tries to justify a high salary every ten minutes. The amount of responsibility given to the secretary is instructive and so is her calibre. In practice the coach will spot which areas are particularly sensitive; he will apply pressure where he feels the manager is open to suggestion and still likely to pay the fee. Individual coaching is the art of the possible but a surprising amount is possible.

Short sessional coaching

In more normal coaching, the coach spends shorter periods, say one to three hours at a time, with one to three managers. This is less expensive but the coach has less time to observe; so either the subject must be specific, eg appraisal interviewing, or the coach must take the initiative by asking questions and following a plan.

Appraisal interviewing is a common subject for such coaching, together with writing job descriptions, target setting etc, because it is usually necessary for an adviser to help individual managers in the first two or three instances, no matter how well the general principles were explained at an initial meeting. Nobody knows all the questions to ask until he has put the procedure into practice. Less commonly, an adviser sits in at some appraisal interviews, having coached the superior before hand; he then analyses the session afterwards. A third party inhibits what is already an embarrassing process, but such interviews are unlikely to be well conducted without practice and improvement is more likely with feed-back from an impartial witness. The observer can open the meeting by referring to the potential embarrassment and thereby reduce it.

There are many examples of coaching in a procedure. Cost accountants explain their budget forms and sales managers their reporting procedures. A consultant putting in MBO is probably the most familiar example of coaching by an outsider, but the method is applicable whenever an hour can be set aside for a particular subject and a practical session.

The subjects suitable for such coaching are those where the points that can be made by a lecturer seem obvious, and it is not until a manager tries to apply them that practical snags arise. A typical manager might say 'The general principles of budgeting are easy enough, but I cannot see how they would help me; besides, I cannot really give firm figures because of the number of variables and uncertainties in my situation'. The same is true of defining key-result areas, explaining budget variances and writing reports. Whenever the practice is more difficult than the theory, coaching is appropriate. The technique is to explain the principles briefly, probably to a group; the coach then sits with each manager while he prepares his first budget, for example. This is training in the real situation and the purpose and relevance are immediately seen.

Coaching is possible on a wider basis than procedures and techniques, and the coach can question the manager with the aim of helping him to sort out priorities and realize any inconsistences or areas not thought through. The technique of the supplementary question is again appropriate; the skill lies in avoiding an inquisitorial image at one extreme and being unwilling to touch on sensitive areas at the other. The emphasis of the interview must be on helping the manager, not on showing how clever the coach is. A good suggestion is one which provokes the response 'That is a good idea, I had not thought of that.' The aim during a one hour session should be to leave the manager with one or two ideas he wants to pursue further. Success is measured by the thoughts the manager acts upon.

Subjects suitable for this type of coaching session are those where line managers typically have neither time nor incentive to think things through. Priorities, career plans and the range of questions covered by the self assessment form (Figure 2) are examples. Another line of enquiry is to ask about problems, to see if any are recurrent or if there might be an unsuspected common cause. If you ask a manager about his problems, the chances are that he will quote you three from the last 24 hours, but this is a starting point: you can ask if any have occurred before, whether he asked anybody for help, whether he thought of enough possible solutions etc. Alternatively, you can ask him what decisions he has taken in the last few days, what process he went through and why he made the choice he did. You will be bound to discover some assumptions which have not been challenged for some time, and you will get the answer 'experience' in reply to some question about how he knew what to do: these are areas to probe gently—trying to uncover alternatives but remembering that too harsh a pressure will produce the opposite of learning.

It might therefore be a useful tactic to begin by discussing problems, or where the manager wants to go, as the two subjects he is likely to be most expansive about, or relationships up, down and sideways. Once you produce a response, the manager will enjoy the session, and this will happen after you have planted (by question or suggestion) an idea that appeals to him. The extent to which he will enjoy an intellectual debate or cross-examination will vary from man to man and so will the willingness to pour out troubles, complaints or bravado. The coach must adjust his style accordingly. Sometimes listening sympathetically can provide a worthwhile safety valve; if a manager has too much on his mind to think objectively, a short release session might be all that can be achieved. You can often provide more positive therapy by asking: 'Why don't you do something about it?' 'What could you do on your own initiative?' This should lead either to action or some softening of the complaint, or possibly to revelation of the true complaint. Do not attempt too much in early sessions and be satisfied if you get commitment to two action points. In an ideal session, both parties spark suggestions off the other and the manager uses the coach as a sounding board. The two way exchange is ideal but takes time to achieve.

Coaching teams

Coaching of a working group is likely to focus on its methods of working together. The coaching might be specific, eg on committee procedures, decision making etc, or seeking to expose and eliminate any faults in 'group process' which will be explained later.

The early methods of group coaching are now rather out of favour. Once, the consultant would sit through a normal committee meeting and criticize at the end. He would point to woolliness of objectives, people going off the point, talking simultaneously and not minuting who was to do what. The coach was rarely at a loss for something to say but, by confronting a working group so directly, he was likely to unite them in the resolve to ignore him when he had gone. There is a case for one member of the committee counting the instances of over-talking, and recording who talked to whom and how often, but that is a later stage, when self-teaching is established.

Better use can be made of an outside observer at committees if he leads a discussion of issues like chairmanship, the responsibility of others to help the chairman, minute-taking and committee procedure. Another legitimate use of team coaching is to follow up something like the external Kepner—Tregoe[1] or Coverdale[2] courses. The managers who attend the courses acquire some concepts and a vocabulary,

[1] Courses on problem solving and decision making by Kepner–Tregoe, Christmas Lane, Farnham Common, Slough, Bucks.
[2] Coverdale Training, courses in self-development of individual managers or effective teams. Training Partnerships, 56 Denison House, London, S.W.1.

but they need help in explaining them to colleagues and in applying them in practice. The role of the coach therefore is to help translate actual problems into the concepts that have been taught; this may sound a limited role, but such interpretation and follow-up is essential to the success of an externally learned technique.

As usually understood, team training does not confine itself to regular committees but takes a team that works together (either a boss and his team or managers on the same level who interact) and gives them practice in working together. The initial work may be done in a hotel and the group work on a series of tasks. Tower building with children's bricks has been well publicized and is one of several deliberately simple opening exercises: so simple that participants can do it with half their brain while the other half studies how the group is tackling the task. If you began by coaching on issues of major importance, everyone would be too involved to be objective either about his own role or about the group as a whole. The technique is to begin with simple and enjoyable exercises that are non-threatening and non-emotional, and to get the group to review its performance at the end of each task. It then becomes aware of group 'process' and, in doing so, can make plans to improve. The next task provides opportunity for that improvement, and the habit of process review is the key to learning. Another technique is to have one member taking no part in each task (a different member each time): the observer sees most and learns most, and can lead the review if the group doesn't realise or won't admit where it fell down.

The sort of faults that groups become aware of are not just the obvious ones like over-talking, talking too long and off the point and leadership struggles. They realize how little listening normally takes place (listening as opposed to not talking), the fact that if somebody is criticized he will switch off for at least ten minutes and how often, after an hour's discussion, there are still differing interpretations of the objective. It takes practice under guidance to realize the importance of listening and showing that you have listened, of supporting and building on other people's suggestions and of keeping quiet unless one can positively help the group towards its objective. A mature group will have resolved internal conflicts and learned who is good at generating new ideas and who is good at spotting genuine difficulties; it will have learned what sort of problems call for tight chairmanship and who makes such a chairman, which call for imagination and therefore for loose chairmanship, and leadership will be passed to the most appropriate person for the task in hand. Nervous energy will be expended only on the task in hand and process review will have become a habit. There is a satisfaction in belonging to such a group that makes the initial self discipline worthwhile in terms of enjoyment as well as productivity. Once at that stage, the group can keep itself up to scratch; it is the job of the coach to get it to that stage.

As this is largely a self-teaching situation, the role of the coach is a catalytic one. He will teach the idea of process review, set the initial 'childish' tasks and ride out whatever storms of protest arise. Depending on what lessons the team draws from its exercises, the coach will introduce the group to the principles of being systematic, of support and building on strengths, and of setting success criteria in advance so that a group can measure if it has achieved its objectives. The coach's main role is to set up the situation from which the group draws its own conclusions; he will be needed less and less, although follow through is never automatic. The best disciplined teams can go out of control over time or under pressure; they may not realize that the principles apply not just in committees but whenever the members interact with one another. The coach should end up with a watching brief.

A more interventionist form of coaching is known as process consultation. This is one of the tools of Organization Development (OD, see Chapter 11) consultants, who help firms to understand individual and group pyschological processes. A process consultant takes no part in the technicalities of the discussion but may intervene from time to time to comment on how the group is behaving, and may draw attention to psychological factors like the defence mechanisms (see Chapter 3). For example, if Mr X was opposing something strongly, but not very convincingly, the consultant might ask whether he was really expressing anxiety that the proposed change might lessen the value of his own experience and qualifications. That would be a harsh intervention, but things are often said which are illogical and explicable only as expressions of a deeper, and possibly quite distant, fear or resentment. The process coach will help the group to become aware of them.

He will also raise individual and group issues which, while being common stumbling blocks to change, are not normally discussed openly. He will help the group to understand their conflicts both within the group and between them and outsiders. The OD consultant helps them to understand their inner motivations and his skill is in knowing how deeply (in the sense of exposing personal and emotional issues) to intervene. The T-group trainer also gets people to discuss personal fears and animosities and to tell other members of the group what they really think of them. It is a measure of the sophistication of a firm how much openness, candour and 'levelling' takes place between managers in conflict because such tensions, if not released, limit individual as well as group performance.[1]

The initial learning of behavioural concepts and the initial loosening up may best be done away from work, ideally among strangers, but the 'pay off' comes when managers apply their new concepts to themselves and their work: this needs a well qualified coach in attendance. Training in the real situation will meet the normal resistances to change so there is a good case for teaching how to handle, or at least understand, them as a first step.

Coaching in coaching

Practice in coaching is difficult because the behavioural

[1] *T Group Training.* ATM Occasional Paper No. 2, ed. Whitaker G, Blackwell, 1965.

areas can be explosive for beginners. The larger firms of OD consultants can train their trainers by letting them observe several groups to start with and then giving them limited tasks under the supervision of an experienced man. Internal coaches are best trained by an outside consultant if there are no experienced men in the firm: you can teach yourself how to make groups aware of their own process but behavioural interventions are not for the amateur.

Coaching line managers in how to coach their subordinates presents the main problem. This is difficult in one sense because the best coaching is turning unexpected situations to good account; you cannot therefore arrange to sit in on such a session. You can sit in on some formal coaching sessions, or you can simply ask what coaching has taken place in the last week or two. While observing, check that the atmosphere is one of help rather than criticism and, if you are in a position to do so, ask to see the classification of delegated duties referred to in Chapter 3. The list of decision areas where the subordinate must consult before acting should reduce over six months and this is a measure of coaching as well as delegation.

The first step in coaching coaches is to get the atmosphere right—relaxed, open and supportive. Once coaching happens managers are likely to ask for help, and it is relatively easy to arrange small group meetings at which general principles and individual difficulties are discussed. The actual coaching techniques that need to be imparted are relatively few and simple, but the organizational spirit is critical: it is particularly pointless to play with coaching until you have got that right.

5 Projects

Planned experience and coaching are ways of using a manager's actual situation as a learning vehicle: projects supplement these and are the principal media for broadening experience. Projects are still real in that there is nothing hypothetical about them and the best ones have a significance for the firm as well as for the 'trainee'. The fatal mistake is to set something up as a 'training exercise', but a significant project will catch the imagination of the team and the various conditions for learning apply, namely:

relevance is visible

they can build on their existing experience

somebody is to take note of the project and their performance.

A good project for a cross-functional team is ideally one that will make the team look at several, if not all, functions while gathering facts and considering possible recommendations. A project with long term as well as company wide implications provides the best development; it also shows up who has the potential to consider matters from larger perspectives and who continues to represent his department's view. It is useful if trainees have to interview suppliers or, better still, people in the customer chain—there is no better way of getting a new insight into one's own firm.

Projects generate their own momentum (this may take some time if the 'reality' is not appreciated at first) and a great deal of energy and private time can be put in. If cleverly designed, the project will enable the trainees to develop without realizing it; they will learn from each other as well as asking for specific help from their tutor. This is the equivalent of the school visit which provokes children to ask questions: it is the correct way to put across theory, ie in response to a conscious need.

How to select the team

The first decision is between individual and team projects. Other things being equal a team is better, especially when drawn from different functions, because the participants learn from each other and learn about working as a team while tackling the project. Reasons for choosing an individual project might include the impossibility of releasing people from several functions or one manager with a particular development need. There might be only one or two men available in a small firm but a more acceptable argument for a one man project might be the need to train, say, a general manager designate. With induction, it is better to set up projects instead of inviting the new man to sit by various Nellies or trying to tell him all he needs to know. Induction projects are widely used for graduate trainees but they could be used at much higher levels, the justification being the principle that people learn much better, when they have a purpose than when they are just watching, listening or asking questions randomly.

Many individual projects are like method study investigations: it is well known how the need to record what is happening sharpens observation and having to suggest alternatives sharpens the critical faculties. Now that job enrichment is making us retreat from work simplification and the extreme divisions of labour, method study is almost in disfavour, but it remains invaluable as a mental discipline and a training tool. The approach is not confined to the factory floor and, in selecting an individual for such a project, you would often choose someone from a different function; lack of prior knowledge (and prejudice) can help the investigation as well as, by definition, helping the trainee. This type of project is valuable for a variety of people: the high fliers, obviously, but also the uncritical and parochial. Having had a new idea in another function, they might have one in their own.

Team projects should be the norm, cross-functional when possible. More than six amounts to a major co-ordination exercise in itself (above and beyond the instructive difficulties) but the ideal team would be four or five people from different functions. This results not so much in the marketing men learning accounting techniques as in learning how accountants approach problems, and how they have to qualify their answers. (Engineers and accountants are usually equally horrified about how imprecise the other's function turns out to be.) One of the benefits the participants will mention afterwards is the chance to get to know X better. They may well have dealt with X for years, say by monthly telephone calls, but have only a rough idea of how he ticks. Wrong ideas and irrational dislikes of people in other functions are common; it is more important to discover that accountants are human, even if not the most extrovert or adventurous, than it is to know the subtle distinction between debits and credits. The common weakness in communications is as broad as this and is not a question of being secretive or unable to write clearly: we don't try to communicate with people we don't understand.

Within the cross-functional team, it by no means follows that the accountant should handle the mathematical aspects, although when under time pressure this is likely. Equally, the internal organization of the team is part of the task and the initial team building exercises may help to find out individual strengths.

Mixing ranks can be a mistake, both because of prejudging the internal leadership and, unless the firm has a history of such openness, the senior men in the team feel exposed and obliged to take a strong lead or dramatically do the opposite. Problems can arise from including managers at different stages of their development: a group of high fliers between 28 and 35 is excellent, as is a bunch of backbone managers who are on a project whose purpose is to make them look into the offices adjacent to their own; to mix the two types would produce such differences of individual purpose as to make agreed action unlikely.

How to generate projects

If an organization accepts the theoretical justification for projects as a major tool for developing managers, the question of how to select the project arises. There is rarely a shortage of project material as every firm has investigations it would like to make but has never got round to, policies that haven't been rethought for some years and assignments it is thinking of giving to consultants. The problem is not shortage of projects, or even the difficulty of defining them, but both team members and top management need considerable education in what is possible (because of the misconceptions and prejudices about training). A common attitude to training can be illustrated by a certain managing director who said that his managers were very busy at present: one major product was becoming obsolete, a firm he had taken over was producing a clash of management styles and there was a short term liquidity problem. 'We shall have solved these problems in about six months time,' he said, 'and then we shall be ready for some training.' In other words, three ideal teaching projects were staring him in the face, and demonstrable management short-comings, but he had not realized that training might help his top managers and that the best vehicles for it were precisely the problems he had outlined.

The best projects are chosen by the project team themselves but the tutor will probably have to make the first one or two selections. He may well choose something relatively simple first because of the importance of an early feeling of success: something of positive benefit, no matter how small, which does not tread on any senior toes might be implemented quickly and so prove that the projects were genuine. An example of biting off an easily digested mouthful came from an investigation into high staff turnover in certain schools. The recommendation was that new members of staff spend a day in the buildings, with travel expenses paid, before their first day teaching, so that they could familiarize themselves with the geography and the spirit of the school. This was a relatively small problem, serious to the new teachers but unsuspected in the hierarchy, with a simple solution entailing little expense and no skin off any individual noses. The resulting success lead to enthusiasm and the possibility of playing for higher stakes next time.

There are some safe bets for initial projects. One is the management of time (of which more in Chapter 9); when a working group has analysed its own use of time, it is usually alive both to the need to improve and to suggestions that are within its own competence to implement. Lack of discipline in committees can be easily demonstrated, eg by a tape recorder, and can form another good project subject. Another possibility (and a sign of the times?), is to simplify the information system in a given area so that the manager would actually use it. In other words, a tutor new to a firm would pick areas of universal weakness such as these; an inside man could make a more informed choice of areas susceptible to improvement by collective effort.

While it is important to have an early success, it is also important to tackle something major at a relatively early stage. If a major decision was imminent, there would be no harm in getting the development team to present its recommendations, even if its solution was not accepted; a proposed merger, a reorganization or a specification for a new product might come into this category. Questions of this degree of importance and confidentiality are used in the famous Reed 'Chairman's Cadre' training,[1] where it is a principle to give managers problems normally dealt with at much higher levels. It is fatal to set up a long range planning committee and to deny it access to all the financial information or to call in a large firm of consultants to propose a reorganization, discuss it at board level, and then announce a *fait accompli* to management. An organization change is of vital

---

[1] The Chairman's Cadre is a well known system of intensive training for high fliers designed by Sir Don Ryder of Reed International.

interest to everybody and needs no stimulus to get discussion going. Whether or not the project team's recommendations were accepted would not be critical but implementation of the new structure could be a further project which would start from a basis of understanding and commitment. In spite of today's propaganda against authority, most managers are willing to carry out instructions they disagree with, providing they have had the chance to put their own case and have been properly listened to.

Therefore use something of major importance as a project as soon as possible. If none is available, tackle a problem that would mean spending or saving at least £20,000. This might be a capital expenditure, a different discount structure or a major elimination of paperwork. Top professional managers regularly take decisions involving sums of money many times larger than their own salary: questions of equivalent importance should be given to project teams to take the awe out of such figures. If there is the will to set real projects, generating them should not be difficult.

You will obviously tailor projects to your people and your problems. What would stretch high fliers would be wrong elsewhere. If your purpose was to give some backbone managers a better view of how their job fitted in to the firm as a whole, and to give them some new stimulation, set a project which focuses on the inter-relationships between three or four fairly close departments. If there is plenty of inter-departmental understanding, possibly at the cost of too many committees, then look at committee procedures or at which standing committees could meet less often. If there is too much sticking to the rules, discuss when it would be justified to break them. If you have an excess of managerial talent, look at possible diversifications to utilize it. It should be possible to find areas of investigation to meet both company and individual needs. The tutor's skill lies in finding the right people and the right general areas: if he does that well, he will soon be in a monitoring role only.

How to monitor projects

Once projects get properly underway they will vary of their own accord so the question arises how, if at all, they should be monitored and what sort of inputs would be helpful. Ideally, the project team asks for assistance with a particular technique or advice on presentation, but is it sufficient to do nothing if nothing is asked of you?

One acceptable and instructive form of monitoring is to have more than one project team and allow them to criticize each other's progress at, say, fortnightly intervals. This produces all the necessary questions like 'have you thought about . . . .' and saves the tutor from a pernickety role. If numbers are too few for the luxury of rival project teams and assuming that projects are part-time, ie additional to normal jobs, and are spread over two to three months, the tutor will need to keep in touch with what is happening. It is the mark of a mature group that they tell the tutor to disappear but, as his honour is at stake, what can he do?

He can get the team to make a presentation to him at intervals, thus making them reappraise where they are going and probably see for themselves which areas need further investigation. It will be fairly easy for the tutor to make suggestions about presentation, and ways of displaying the existing situation, and to comment on the thought processes. His comments might incorporate the skills of a problem solving tutor or a process consultant as discussed in 4.2 or he might simply ask for more alternatives to be generated before the team leaped to its conclusion.

It is not easy to strike a balance between doing nothing and doing so much that it is resented as interference. The tutor should probably err in the former direction and so structure the situation (for example, by making sure that the managing director is known to be going to attend the final presentation) that the team will set itself high standards, be self-critical and ask for advice. The tutor must not let the team put forward half-baked proposals or, if he does, it must be to administer a deliberate shock to a group that is either complacent or too ready in its solutions. The tutor's

49

function is to make sure that the project does not fizzle out for any reason (and the most trivial pretexts have been seized on in early stages), to intervene as little as possible, to give or arrange for help when requested, and to maintain the right amount of pressure so that the team sets itself high standards and sweats, but doesn't die.

How to appraise projects

The short answer to how to review projects is to treat them as if they weren't development projects: they should be given exactly the same consideration that they would get if the proposals were coming from consultants or an internal investigatory team. If a proposal for spending £35,000 on capital equipment would normally be decided by the managing director and the other executive directors, that body should review the presentation. It would be as wrong to accept a proposal, without going into it in detail because it was a training exercise, as it would be to tear it apart in order to keep the juniors in their place. Proper review is as much a development activity for board members as it is for the project team, as the top team knows its decision will be scrutinized and that any refusal will have to be carefully justified if the morale of the project team is not to be broken for ever.

It is a revolutionary suggestion, but the directors should make their counter-proposal to the project team. That would be good development all round and would ensure that the decision was not taken for inadequate reasons and then hushed up on grounds of confidentiality or 'only we are wise enough to decide this.'

Presentations should be made to whoever has authority to implement the proposals. I would suggest a verbal presentation, backed up by appropriate visual aids and with as many of the team taking part as possible. A verbal presentation gives practice in a range of skills, in which most managers are very willing to accept help, and also adds an element of drama and purpose to the investigation. A written report is desirable in addition, or at least a summary of conclusions, so that the team has a record of what it did and, if top management asks for time before making a decision, the facts are recorded.

The manner of review is critical to the success of subsequent development projects. Until the first proper review there will be scepticism that, because the projects are a training activity, they are not genuine; they will be seen as a chore and possibly done half-heartedly. Once it is seen that top management is not going to shelter behind its status, and that the project team can influence things on the ground the credibility gap will be bridged and the full power of management training in the real situation will be released.

Section II

The difficulties and how to overcome them

6 Difficulties

Training in the real situation causes many more problems than external courses and hypothetical case studies: as was said in the introductory pages of this publication, the case for it lies in its potential effectiveness. The problems are such that an organization cannot pay lip service to the idea; it must be done properly or not at all; this means facing the difficulties and being aware of the fundamental differences between this approach to training and the others.

Real resistances

The first difference between training in the real situation and in the hypothetical is that you run into real resistance. If a man is sent on a course, he may worry about why he was thought to need it but at least his bosses can sleep comfortably. If a project team is looking at the production area, it may well propose change and that will threaten the production director, who may try to sabotage the exercise. He can do this directly by attacking the exercise (or the tutor), indirectly by witholding information or passively by seeing that the investigation stops at a suitable distance from whatever he is sensitive about. All projects are likely to propose change and to upset somebody, and he may well be very senior. He will feel an implied criticism and erect defence mechanisms. Project teams normally want to investigate areas like the organization structure, marketing strategy or diversification, which the board has normally considered that it alone is competent to discuss.

All the resistance to change resists training in the real

situation but there can be additional, deeper reasons for opposition. It is all too common for the top managers to be less able than their juniors (one can speculate idly on the reasons: they were not fit enough to go to the war or were promoted during the selling boom of the 1950s) and, consciously or subconsciously they will resist development projects which will demonstrate how good their juniors are and improve them still further. In particular, parallel investigation of the same question as previously suggested would be out of the question. Training in the real situation requires that the senior managers are senior on merit and therefore have a genuine interest in developing their subordinates.

Pressure of time

The most obvious difficulty of training in the real situation is that it adds to what already feels like an overload of work. The feeling of time pressure is more important than the absolute amount of time involved. Managers always have something they want to do urgently: all are short of time, many to the extent of feeling stress because they can never catch up. Besides, if they can find the time for their training exercises too easily, this will seem to be an admission that they were under-occupied before.

Training in the real situation will occupy at least 10 per cent of a manager's time, which does not sound an unreasonable amount to devote to self-improvement and improving the contribution of one's job; in practice, half a day a week is difficult to find. If people are given projects in addition to their normal jobs, as opposed to being released full-time for a course, they have to make 10 per cent if not 20 per cent of their time available. Individual coaching is time-consuming and team coaching entails taking time to discuss objectives and later to review how each decision was arrived at, all of which seem a waste of time when met for the first time.

In-company training has been known to fail because the amount of time required was not foreseen; this is a particular danger in the early months before the successes have been felt. If a project team gets its teeth into its task, it is not unusual for the total time spent to shoot over 10 per cent, but then the morale is high and the time is found from somewhere. In the opening months, proposals for training activities will meet the cry, 'I haven't time, I'm already doing a full time job and . . .' Shortage of time is the easiest excuse for opting out of training and unfortunately it usually contains a measure of truth. The plan for training has therefore to include a plan to overcome this objection.

Individual differences in motivation

Differences in the motivations of managers being developed can pose problems. It cannot be assumed that all managers have the long term good of the organization as their prime aim, or even that their wish for promotion is strong. Any group contains some self-starters, some who talk about being ambitious but don't quite deceive themselves, some who are flaccid and contented and some who have something to hide. A project team which contains a mix of motivations, including both offensive and defensive personalities, is a difficult group team to weld into a vehicle for action.

It is relatively easy to get enthusiasm in a project team composed of high-fliers, in a firm which is expanding fast enough to accommodate all of them. A more limited project for backbone managers will strike them as interesting and non-threatening. Just as development needs are particular to individuals and their psychological make-up, the planning of training must take differences of motivation into account, also personal animosities and the all-important relationships with immediate superiors. Problems arise in planning group activities because the needs of the members must be compatible. Different motivation is a reality of life with which groups must learn to deal, but that is an advanced lesson.

Initial feeling of impotence

Many training exercises meet with little initial enthusiasm

because nobody believes anything will change. 'Why should we bother setting out our thoughts on this, when old . . . will never listen?' is a common reaction. Similar feelings occur in groups of managers who agree on the desirability of a change but see little point in putting it forward. A feeling of impotence is surprisingly prevalent among middle managers. They feel that their recommendations would not get a proper hearing or they would not be allowed to look at certain areas, and this reaction is common even when their seniors are in fact open to suggestion. Managers at all levels have a tendency to regard themselves as prisoners of their situation (partly because this is an excuse for not trying harder to change things), either because their boss is inflexible, somebody is unreasonable or the organization structure is cramping and immutable. Organizations are sometimes inflexible, but often managers have not fully explored the boundaries of their authority (even when confronted by an apathetic top management which, by definition, would probably let them get away with murder).

As a result of this feeling of collective powerlessness, whether justified or not, the first suggestion that a training exercise should set out to change the real situation meets with disbelief. It is not just that the habit of regarding training as something apart is so deeply ingrained, but, as Alistair Mant[1] said in a less publicized section of his report, 'Managers need to be shown, over a period of time, that they can influence their situation.' Initially, managers who would discuss case studies fluently will not see any point in discussing—as opposed to moaning about—their own situation. This assumed impotence does not sound like a training need in traditional terms but, when it exists, it must be tackled before any impetus can be generated.

Lack of glamour

To quote Mant[1] again, his reference to attendance at some outside courses as 'accolades' reflects the prestige attaching to certain training institutions. Managers are pleased to be

[1] MANT, A, *The Experienced Manager, op cit*, pp 10, 39.

chosen to go; they feel that having attended in itself increases their market worth.

It is my belief that training in the real situation is the most effective means of training, to be supplemented but not replaced by outside courses. So far it lacks any glamour or universally recognized 'accolade'. This means that managers are not automatically pleased at being selected and, when they discover they are going to have to find half a day a week and write up their activities, for example, their initial attitude is one of suspicion if not resentment. All training is approached with a degree of fear but in-company development has no sugar on the pill: this is another problem to be overcome.

7 Some unfreezing devices

'Unfreezing devices' is a rather loosely defined but picturesque term. It can be defined as the loosening of attitudes necessary before any development can begin, in particular, the attitude that 'This training or theory does not apply to me'. The early stages of a development scheme are the most vital and the most difficult. If managers feel that they personally are managing as well as possible in the face of immutable difficulties, they are not likely to volunteer for training exercises which will take 15 per cent of their time. Equally, if their shortcomings are brutally revealed, defence mechanisms will close their minds to suggestions and once again no learning will take place.

If the learner feels he already knows the truth and either doesn't see the need or doesn't want to spend time considering new 'truths', some way must be found of getting him to lower his defences and wanting to learn before he will really listen. This unfreezing process is sometimes likened to a disturbance of equilibrium and the metaphor is useful because it allows the learner to 'refreeze' and assimilate the lesson after seeking and testing alternative methods to restore his equilibrium.

It is worth repeating the basic points of adult learning because all the requirements must be met during the unfreezing stage. To quote Lovin and Casstevens,[1] managers will learn only when:

they recognize a lack or a need in themselves

[1] Lovin, B C and Casstevens, E R. *Coaching, Learning and Action.* American Management Association, 1972.

they identify what would help them

they want what is needed (ie they see it as directly helpful to themselves)

they take steps to acquire it

In other words, the unfreezing stage must show managers that they could do better, how to acquire the skill, for example, and how to put it into practice. It helps to make the exercise enjoyable. Self-discovery techniques have a large part to play and the aim must be to lead managers to discover their existing weaknesses and also to give them a feeling of improvement almost straight away. It is against these quite stringent requirements that the following unfreezing devices are discussed.

Diary keeping

Diary keeping is a safe bet. Virtually any manager who has kept a diary for one or two weeks is quite shaken by the results. The implications are seen privately and gradually, and that produces the unfreezing. As Drucker[1] has said, most managers do not know where their time goes. Typically, they know they are subject to interruptions, but are appalled to see how many: they know their time is fragmented but think their boss is the main source of interruptions; often it turns out to be a host of people on the same level. The amount of time spent in social chit-chat is not written down, but the lesson is taken inwardly, as is the fact that one is not managing one's situation so much as responding to it. Few managers realize how rarely they devote a solid half hour to one problem and how few decisions of any importance they take.

It is not my purpose to go into the better use of time, but keeping a diary is important as an eye-opener and most managers make one or two private resolves to do something differently. My suggested diary form (Figure I) is designed for general unfreezing purposes. The interval of a quarter of an hour is difficult to keep but it is the most accurate and

[1] DRUCKER, P. *The Effective Executive*, Heinemann, 1967.

becomes a habit more easily than, say, recording once an hour. You may prefer to design a less fearsome looking form, or to use the 'System Frekvensor',[1] an electronic desk device which bleeps at random intervals and you punch a card to show your activity at the time. The cards are fed into a computer for analysis. Alternatively, Rosemary Stewart shows some more refined forms in *Managers and Their Jobs*,[2] which can be used for further analysis when an area of weakness has been exposed. For initial unfreezing, self analysis is essential, followed ideally, by group discussion.

It is particularly effective to get a working team to do the exercise simultaneously. Their mutual banter helps to get the diaries filled in but, more important, they can then discuss the points that emerge and make their own plans for improvement. When the whole team has realized the importance of time and how much they affect each other's use of it, they are usually prompted to make some experiments. The suggestions will vary from group to group, but might include an hour when the internal telephone is banned, a closing time for meetings as well as a starting time, not dropping in on each other whenever an idea occurs, or cutting out social chit-chat except on Fridays. When the group discussion leads into planning and implementation, unfreezing and feelings of immediate improvement are both present. No teaching has taken place but the ideal conditions for learning have been met.

Self assessment

It might seem surprising that a form which asks managers to assess their own development needs can achieve anything useful. If a simple question was asked on its own, it probably would not achieve anything. But the purpose of the questionnaire shown in Figure 2 is to take the manager through a considerable self analysis so that he is better in-

[1] System Frekvensor, a Swedish desk device with electronic signal at random intervals for diary keeping and subsequent computer analysis. Distributed in the UK by London University Computing Services, 39 Gordon Square, London, W.C.1.

[2] STEWART, R. Managers and their Jobs, *op. cit*, chapter 8.

formed about himself, if not chastened, by the time he gets to the question on training needs. The power of the questionnaire may not be apparent at first sight; the first few answers can be taken straight from a Key Results Sheet (if MBO is in operation), and it might well be thought that every manager knows his own career plan and regales his wife nightly with his strengths and achievements. Surprisingly often, the line manager does not give much thought to studying his own career, and its progress, or even finding out if the firm has a plan for him. The question, 'What have you achieved in the last twelve months?' hits several managers below the belt and the exercise has been known to produce visible change (see Case Study 3). Again, it is the self analysis that is important and it may help in some firms to announce that nobody will look at the answers.

The discipline of studying where one is going, looking at progress to date, in terms of skills acquired as well as promotion, and considering what is still needed turns out to be a three or four hour job. Experienced managers ought to be able to rattle the answers off but usually they can't; in realizing this, they often recognize that they have been pursuing their daily tasks and crises so hard that they have lost sight of their personal long term objectives.

Self diagnosed needs are not trivial. Most people without accountancy experience feel this to be a serious deficiency and those accountants who have managerial ambitions feel they ought to know something about marketing. Anybody who aspires to general management is likely to be aware of one or two areas he should know more about. It may help to get informed answers to give a manager extra information before setting the questionnaire, say by getting him to take part in a group dynamics exercise, to give a talk or to spend half a day in a different department. Properly informed and stimulated, a manager's self assessed training needs will provide an adequate starting point.

The form in Figure 2 was designed to be administered by an outside consultant, who would follow it up with an individual meeting. An outsider may get honest answers more easily and the interview elicits much that would not be committed to paper. The questionnaire can be used internally provided that there is sufficient trust in the person administering it. There is no absolute need for the interview but it is probably helpful to talk through the answers with somebody who is relatively impartial.

The questionnaire must be followed quickly by something relevant, such as a project or instruction in an area shown to be of interest. The strength of an unfreezing device is the extent to which it provokes a desire for action: self assessment will provoke the opportunity, and the necessity, to get some training action under way quickly. It is so powerful a tool that it would be dangerous not to meet any of the desires it brings to the surface.

Behavioural packages

Many of the packaged residential courses provide useful unfreezing devices. It is expensive to put all senior and middle managers through such courses but the object is fairly complex, ie to provoke a fundamental rethink of basic attitudes and philosophies, and there may be no easier or cheaper way of doing this. It may be preferable to send the top men to separate public courses of the same package, so that they can let their psychological hair down in front of strangers. This can be followed by a Phase II exercise run specially for a working team.

Part of unfreezing is to see ourselves as others see us. Most sales training and public speaking courses now use closed circuit television as a way of doing that literally: the results are horrifying, but instructive. Some courses on decision-making begin by recording a group discussion and playing it back. Again, the group realizes how it went off at tangents, leapt to assumptions and missed vital points. Unfreezing takes place in an uncomfortable but acceptable way. Such courses have the wider benefit of showing people their shortcomings in what they thought was an area mastered long ago, and the better ones (eg Kepner-Tregoe)[1] provide a

[1] See p 15.

structure for students to employ when they get back to their own jobs.

Most of the packages are behavioural. Their main purpose is to explore management philosophies or group process but they all have an unfreezing element. They vary in the intensity of pain produced from T-groups, where anything goes, and Blake's Grid (Phase I) where members write on a blackboard what the others think about them, to Coverdale Training[1], where direct criticism is barred and the emphasis is on strengths and successes. A common result of these packages is that people are aware of how they come across to others, and how what they do and say is helpful or not to the group. A residential week has the advantage of giving members the chance to experiment and to improve during the week. Thus having had their confidence somewhat shaken in the early stages, their morale is lifted by the end and they make plans to use their new knowledge.

The general structure of the Blake and Reddin[2] grids is to provide participants with a series of concepts such as character types, managerial styles, defence mechanisms and intra- and inter-group conflicts; the group is then given practice in applying these concepts to case studies, practical exercises or films and finally to themselves. The group exercises provide sufficiently realistic situations for people to show their true colours; how people behave in a group situation under stress is more important to their managerial effectiveness than any technique or coldly analytical skill. Self awareness in these areas is valuable and is bound to shake even the most senior manager out of any complacency.

Each course has its own message to put across and most have their own follow-up modules, but they can all be valuable preliminaries for any programme of real situation training. Which package you chose would depend on how you view their particular messages (one proposes an *ideal* management style, one talks of an *appropriate* management style, another plays down personalities etc) or you could

[1] See p 15.
[2] 3-D theory of Professor W J Reddin.

65

E

design your own residential week. If you chose the latter, and set out to prepare for the problems caused by training in the real situation, you should include the following objectives:

1 participants should discover they are not as good as they thought
2 several opportunities be given to improve whatever weaknesses are exposed
3 it should be proved that intelligent, well-motivated people do not slip automatically into working well together
4 participants should learn how they come across to others
5 participants should learn to recognize the emotional, psychological and unspoken factors which can hamper group effectiveness; the defence mechanisms that are erected when people are directly criticized or feel threatened, and the difference between what people say, in such circumstances, and what they are sub-consciously expressing
6 the common resistances to change should be analysed
7 participants should be aware of the type of conflicts that arise within a group and between a group and anybody outside it.

In short, there needs to be an awareness of the common reactions and conflicts so that, when coaching or projects produce instances (eg the catalyst is an outsider to the group, projects produce defence mechanisms) the tutor and the team have a common vocabulary and can deal with them. The case study described in Appendix 3 shows the danger of not getting below the surface in the unfreezing stage and not providing quick feelings of success. A well-designed week's programme could provide the answer.

8 Adding purpose

The problem with training is not getting agreement to plans but turning the plans into action. Difficulties arise when a training plan conflicts with a current output target or a senior manager's *amour propre* or, for no particular reason, the trainees themselves lose interest. The trainer is fighting various inertias and neither market competition nor the desire for promotion provide the motivation which might be expected. Against the background of a society of people who want to put their feet up and be entertained, there is a general wish to coast at work, and to avoid anything unpleasant like risk taking, change or, it sometimes appears, thought.

If political and civic apathy are due to the feeling of powerlessness in the face of administration and bureaucracy, managers who are coasting may be doing so because they feel they have no influence on the things that matter. If they were given the chance to shape what concerned them, many might 'switch on' again. The key to getting commitment and motivation, is to prove to managers that they can influence events, and to link this with the development programme. A flexible organization structure would be less cramping; flexible (but monitored) career planning would remove obstacles, and the chance to demonstrate potential would be seized by the ambitious. If these three elements can be combined, as suggested below, then it ought to be possible to release again the forces of self-interest and self-improvement. These forces ought to be powerful motivators and, properly channelled, they could provide the sense of purpose currently lacking in management development.

Develop the organization simultaneously

It is a pity that Organization Development (OD) has a behavioural science connotation because, if managers are working on important projects and producing changes, the organization is being developed—through the development of its managers. What other way is there to make a firm more participative than to get its managers to participate? What better way to decentralize than to get more managers to take decisions? What better way to re-organize to stretch managers than asking them to contribute? As discussed above, projects on weighty subjects make for good personal development as well as organizational improvement and managers find they are not as powerless as they had thought.

Focus your projects on the question of powerlessness. What can be done to make more people feel they are contributing? Tasks can be set to collect information on frustrations and to pool suggestions on what can be changed to offer greater fulfilment. In short, the key to selecting projects is to make the cause of any frustration or apathy the subject of investigation. The more important the projects the more motivation there will be, instead of grumbling about the mess 'they' are making, some (at least) middle managers will be spurred on to attempt constructive suggestions for improvement.

If organizational change is made part of teaching material there is less danger that the head of management development will not be a party to major policy decisions. John Humble[1] has quoted a case of a retail training manager organizing courses for the managers of self-service stores, not knowing that the firm had decided to move into supermarkets. It is important to co-ordinate management development with the corporate plan. If the firm intends to expand by acquisition, it must prepare surplus managerial talent to

[1] HUMBLE, J. Make more of your managers, *Financial Times*, 9 January, 1973.

put into the new companies: creating new divisions will call for more men with general management experience; diversification might call for an entirely different range of experience. The implications for career prospects and the morale of managers should be considered before policy decisions are taken and the head of management development should be a party to them. He is then in a position—as he should be —to develop the organization and the managers simultaneously.

Dynamic succession planning

The opportunity to demonstrate potential is one of the advantages of management training by projects. A common demotivating factor is that ambitious managers feel that nobody is watching them, in the sense of noticing extra effort, or spotting unused abilities.

In an as yet undiscovered section of *Practice of Management*, Drucker[1] said that management development should not aim at replacing today's managers but must focus on the needs of tomorrow. He went on to ask what organization will be needed to attain the objectives of tomorrow, what management jobs, what management qualifications and skills? This approach to succession planning offers another key to momentum.

The approach so far has been rather static. Figure 4 in *Developing Effective Managers* by Tom Roberts[2] is correctly labelled a management replacement chart and shows a typical organization structure with the people who might succeed to each job. It is worth drawing such a chart to cover emergencies; a time dimension can be added by showing retirement and expected transfer dates, and the implication of expected gains, losses and promotions at the different levels of management. Succession charts tend to be shrouded in secrecy and suspicion, especially in small firms, and there is an undertone of waiting for dead or promoted men's shoes.

[1] DRUCKER, P. *The Practice of Management*, Heinemann, 1955, Chapter 15.
[2] ROBERTS, T. J. *Developing Effective Managers*, IPM, 1967.

But if the organization chart is taken as something to be influenced rather than as something fixed, and if the time spans are dictated not by retirement dates but by market opportunity and by managerial growth, this leads to dynamic succession planning—and motivation.

In practical terms this means that the organization structure is not only open to discussion, as suggested in the last section, but is tailored to take advantage of tomorrow's opportunities and to develop managers to the full. There is little doubt that general management positions (ie positions with responsibility for production and sales, and therefore for profit) are the best for stretching managers, and the more such positions there are available for younger managers the better. The cell organization structure quoted by Anthony Jay[1] allows as many people as possible to run their 'own thing' which could be a product, a geographical area or an advisory function. This not only allows more people to run something but to run it their own way, eg by going for growth or quality, by running on Theory X lines or on a participative basis. Even more important, nobody's progress is limited by questions of relative status, job descriptions or even a boss. Few organizations could run completely on a cell basis (the Dominicans quoted by Jay could only do so because their industry offered no economies of scale) but the aim of the organization structure should be to allow as many managers as possible to develop as far as possible.

If responsibility for his own development is placed with the manager, it follows that he is entitled to suggest what jobs he feels he could do. If they did not have to be in the current chart, that would be so much easier. By definition, one cannot draw a flexible organization or a flexible succession chart: but a dynamic approach to career planning which is not tied to the current structure means that there is everything to play for and this removes the cramping effect of the traditional system.

[1] JAY, A. *Management and Machiavelli*, Hodder and Stoughton, 1967, chapter 9.

Stress role in potential assessment

Trainers are always asked by nervous students at the beginning of programmes, 'Will there be reports to management?'. They are usually given the comforting answer 'No' but I suspect that answer is wrong. The right approach is to say that nobody will be fired for doing badly on projects but that these are an outstanding opportunity to stake a claim for a bigger job. One of the advantages of training in the real situation is that it shows up potential much more effectively than the normal appraisals by a superior, so this is a card to be played strongly when seeking commitment.

Appraisal of potential (as opposed to performance) is subjective and there is always the suspicion that those who give least trouble are rated highest. (The Peter Principle[1] confirms this). Potential appraisal is certainly fallible because:

    higher level jobs call for different types of ability

    there may be a personality clash between manager and superior, they have different types of intelligence, or the superior may be too insecure to give his subordinate a high rating.

    the managers might be in the wrong type of job and not showing up well.

Potential, or the lack of it, is shown in particular by cross-functional projects. It soon becomes apparent who is capable of taking a company-wide and long term view and who continues to represent his department. To respond properly to a project, a manager has to make time available and this means extra delegation or otherwise climbing out of the detail of his current job. The manager without potential responds by saying that he already has a full time job and could he please be released.

The demonstration of potential is to the manager himself and not just to the various observers. But, and this is the big difference, promotions no longer seem to be a mixture of luck, clean noses and mysterious influences: it becomes obvious to everybody who is good at what and promotions

[1] PETER, L J. and HULL, R. *The Peter Principle, op cit.*

evolve by a natural and visibly fair process. What better way to restore the motivation to self-development which is so widely lacking?

9 Sequence for introducing action learning

Obviously the local situation will determine the tactics for making the considerable change to training in the real situation. If you have already gone some way towards it, it will be a question of putting new impetus where needed; if you are starting from scratch, you have certain advantages providing you learn how to use them before it is too late. This chapter should help in either case.

Top level unfreezing

As Bill Reddin[1] has pointed out, it is not necessary for top managers to accept the principles involved in their entirety but it is necessary for them to give time to the programme; time to take part in some exercises, to listen to presentations and to deal with questions that would not otherwise have arisen for four or five years. They must not hit the roof whenever told that a subordinate is 'on the training project' and they must give the scheme a reasonable time to run and prove itself.

Nothing will get far without top management support but, once this type of development is under way, the top managers will be kept up to the mark as a by-product of what their juniors are doing: the problem therefore is to get them sufficiently interested to authorize the expenditure, time and the trouble. The 'work your way upwards by stealth' method or trying to run courses without top man-

[1] Address by Professor W J Reddin at IPM National Conference, 1972.

agement noticing are not helpful approaches. It is equally useless to persuade senior managers to go on prestige summer schools which will flatter them and probably show them one or two techniques they would like to impose. Their informed support for real situation training—or at least informed willingness to give it a try—will be needed at an early stage, and this rules out the 'low profile' approach. So, tell them what you are doing, and get them to take part first.

The easiest case is the chief executive who is genuinely looking for help: you can sell him the idea of something to give a shock to his top management team and prove to them the need for flexibility and re-thinking in unsuspected areas. The chief executive is the number one target; but you can also sell to the two or three most approachable directors the importance of the human assets of the company, and stress that it is their duty to do something to set a lead. The resistances to self-analysis and self-development are emotional: it may therefore be good tactics to use emotional appeals in your attack.

One way or another you must persuade senior managers to take part in some of the unfreezing operations. If they were the first to keep diaries, they would then enjoy seeing that everybody else did so. They could best justify the expense of a three day coaching exercise and this would be good for their internal prestige (apart from whatever they learned). If the entire top management team went to one of the external one week packages, they would find it stimulating and loosening and the common experience would be useful. They might prefer to go separately but they ought then to do something jointly as a second step to build up a common set of concepts and a plan for passing their new awareness downwards.

Spell out difficulties

As difficulties are bound to be encountered with the new approach to development, spell them out in advance. It has always been tempting to pretend that training will be painless and to exaggerate the quantifiable benefits. It is hard enough to sell on the Vent-Axia analogy of something that makes life more pleasant but does not involve anybody in doing anything different, but the subsequent disillusion makes it harder to sell next time. As training in the real situation is bound to produce difficulties and its benefits may or may not show up in the current year, it is only prudent to make this clear from the beginning.

Forewarned is forearmed. Plans can be made to cope with the difficulties, which can then be dealt with according to the plan instead of being unexpected and bringing the whole exercise to an ignominious stop. If you have listed the difficulties in advance you will look wise and in full charge: you lose all dignity if what you promised would be plain sailing does not turn out to be so. Ask senior managers or project teams early on to list the difficulties they can foresee and to prepare contingency plans. Managements are more likely to buy a difficult exercise than an easy miracle because everyone realizes that significant benefits are not obtained without significant effort. So challenge them to prove their virtue by doing something acknowledged to be difficult; above all, do not sell yourself as a 'nice chap' who will rely on the sweet reasonableness of his arguments and the persuasive appeal of his personality. You have a tough role: put it across as such together with your confidence in fulfilling it.

Work on effective use of time

Pressure of time is the most common difficulty facing training in the real situation, whether the difficulty is real, imagined or deliberately generated. There is a good case then for the first project to focus on the use of time. It can be an individual project or, better, a team exercise provoked by diary keeping. When an organization has a number of committees, the focus should be on whether all are necessary, whether they need meet as often and whether they need take as long as they do.

It is not uncommon to release 15 per cent of managers' time as a result of such projects and 10 per cent to 15 per cent is the likely extra load the training activities will put on them. Some people have special difficulties in improving their use of time, eg those in open plan offices or insurance brokers, who spend much time on the telephone; but the higher a man is in the hierarchy, the more discretion he has on how he spends his time and the greater the probability that he will spend it badly.

You should make a fetish of the use of time and should work for the situation where to say 'I haven't time' is acknowledged as an admission of failure. If a manager has been in the same job for over two years, and if he is two levels above foreman, he ought to be so well organized and delegated that routine difficulties are foreseen and headed off by somebody else; he should then have at least 25 per cent of his time free. Get a team to look at any manager who claims he has no time, make lists of those problems which have arisen before, list the new authorities he delegates over three months, note if things go more smoothly when he is absent and generally make his life a misery until he admits either that he has time for development activities or that he is not up to his job.

There is a national need to overcome the presssure of time and the frenzied 'busy-ness' that never seems to improve. This is a problem that will beat you unless you beat it early on. When projects arise out of group diary-keeping, they can be enjoyable and demonstrably productive; therefore play on this with a group of receptive managers and then put pressure on the rest.

Tactics for an established function

In some ways an established department has the harder task. Established training people may feel that affairs are broadly satisfactory (in which case they will resist the whole tenor of this publication), those who realize how little planned improvement of managers has taken place find it difficult if not dangerous to say so to top management. The other difficulties arise because routines will be in existence, though varyingly effective, and line managers and trainers all feel they 'know the score.' Revolution is the last thing anybody expects.

Yet established routines may be the key to making the change. They are often just ticking along, and by-passed when anything significant happens. How often do we hear phrases like 'The appraisal system seems to have served its purpose,' 'MBO is now just another chore,' 'We have had the scheme for 16 years but the appraisals are still sloppy.' One dramatic way of bringing about change is to suspend the routines for a year, to replace them with the self assessment of training needs or to withdraw from all initiatives except to call for each line manager to put forward his own development plan. Alternatively, you can dare a group of senior managers to take part in a diary keeping exercise, or set up a team to investigate something important, without calling it training and possibly without even going near it. Arrange a startling promotion or transfer.

Your aim is to make something happen on the ground and to point out later that this is what training is about, or ought to be. When somebody is promoted because he has shown up well in a project, or when a project leads to a change of policy, management development will be looked at in a new light. Once it is seen to influence careers (in practice) and the organization, its power will be revealed.

Bringing in outside help is the other major step an established department can take. This is often resisted because to ask for consultants to develop managers risks inviting 'I thought I was paying you to do that' from above, and because it seems an admission of failure or a surrender of empire. In fact it is the key to *strengthening* the empire: if the outsider succeeds in loosening attitudes at the top, much more becomes possible everywhere else. Bringing in an outsider is a signal for something new; it provides impetus and may be able to break the disbelief in the possibility of change. I have shown the diversity of competences required for management training in the real situation, so only the very large firms should aim to be entirely self-sufficient and even they must avoid complacency. It is a mark of strength to ask for outside help and to set out what it is to achieve. Finding the right measure of external assistance and establishing it on a permanent and responsible basis is the most hopeful blood-transfusion for a management development department that is established—and taken for granted.

Tactics for a new starter

It is important as a change agent—a new starter, either in an established or brand new department, to realize that you are on trial for the first one or two months: on trial in the sense that line managers are wondering whether or not you are going to count. Their pre-supposition is that you aren't, and if you have not changed anything within two months they will regard that view as confirmed. This rules out any genteel approach such as 'getting the feel of the organization' or the textbook sequence of defining training needs by job descriptions etc, which will change nothing in the first year. While you must not ignore the cultural climate or plunge in recklessly like an MBA[1] in a china shop, as that will unite everyone against you, you must get something moving in the real world: you will then be regarded with awe.

The key is to get something happening, at the seeming initiative of the line managers. If a project arises spontaneously from self-assessments, or you provide some training asked for, no-one can resent you. If a manager learns what he wanted to know or finds himself competent in an unexpected area, he will warm to this unaccustomed responsiveness and relevance of training. The training asked for may not be an entirely correct diagnosis, but it will not be that far wrong. You can always carry out a more complete definition of need later, possibly by setting the drawing of job descriptions as a project. If you can get the right sort of activity under way, it will generate its own momentum and give you time to appreciate the deeper needs of the organization and the individual managers. Get something moving,

[1] Master of Business Administration.

and be theoretical afterwards; that is the way to take an entrance.

You could also make profitable use of an outsider, although it would probably not be sensible to bring in immediate help unless yours was a part-time appointment, in which case the need for impact would outweigh the desirability of establishing yourself in your own right. Once established, bring in extra expertise and muscle-power to coincide with any second wind that the old guard musters when they discover you are changing things.

As a new starter you have one advantage: nobody knows quite what your status is and you have the chance to set your own. Set it high. If you do anything that seems to devalue your status, no matter how prudent, you will never recover it. Act on the assumption that you are advising the managing director on the training of all his managers, including the top ones, seize an early initiative and keep it. The opposite approach, which aims at reaching a position of influence gradually by doing a good job on the foreman first will mean that you never get the top managers in your net, and you will be ineffective.

Section III
Implications

10 Changed role of the trainer

If management training ought to be carried out in the real situation, with additional difficulties on the one hand and far greater potential results on the other, there are wide implications for the trainer and the training function. The changes required could not be more complete: all preconceptions must be removed, the function must be seen and tackled from a different slant and, on the average, higher calibre people are needed.

The old approach

Hitherto, the approach to management training has been for the adviser to analyse needs and make prescriptions. The model of operator training, with its skills analysis and off-the-job training, was translated perhaps too readily into the management field. There is little problem with operator training in identifying the skills required and the trainees are unlikely to argue. There are plenty of cases to prove that if skills are taught in the correct sequence, learning is both quicker and more effective.

The management trainer has so far adopted the same basic assumption that he ought to identify management training needs and to suggest, if not decide, which medicine should be taken in which order. It is not the trainer's ability to diagnose needs that is in question, but the usefulness of the exercise. With the exception of the graduate trainees or supervisors newly promoted into management, the 'trainees' are likely to argue. The most common reaction of managers is that they have no need of training although their boss and certain colleagues could well benefit from some. The trainer has always had a problem with all but the most junior levels of management, a problem all too often solved by not attempting to train them directly and simply circulating course brochures. The difficulties are made worse by something akin to Anthony Jay's[1] distinction between the yogi and the commissar: the trainer is often the more intellectual but this does not give him instant respect from the man of action in production or sales management; natural animosity is the norm, although we rarely say so.

Whether or not the training officer has drawn back from telling managers their training needs, the assumption has been that he ought to. The recommended method of defining training needs by job descriptions and appraisals is only a thin disguise for this reality. In theory, job descriptions are prepared by a manager and his superior; the superior performs the appraisal but, in the early years of any scheme, the adviser usually does about 80 per cent of the task. The adviser usually has to fight to get the system accepted, and he has to go on fighting to get it adhered to. The same is true of proposals for training: most suggestions are made, directly or indirectly, by the adviser. The conflicts between line manager and trainer are all too familiar. Getting appraisals completed, getting people released for courses and getting top management to show interest, are all battles which are familiar, explicable—and lost by the trainer. One possible explanation is that the trainer was wrong to try to be 'prescriptive'; in other words to tell line managers what training they needed. Although he was usually right, conflict and defeat were the likely results. It has been suggested that it is arrogant for the adviser to be prescriptive: I am not sure that this matters: what does matter is the ineffectiveness of trying to push managers further and faster than they want to go.

The new approach

The completely opposite approach would be to train only

[1] JAY, A. *Management and Machievelli, op cit.* chapter 14.

at the request of line managers and to help only in ways which line managers immediately saw as helpful. This would result in some shop floor consultancy, an occasional request for a trainee and some mathematical help in justifying the purchase of a new machine. Simply to ask what training they wanted would get the answer 'None'.

The approach must be such that active co-operation is enlisted: for this, line managers must see the activity as immediately and directly beneficial to themselves. The distinction is rather between being shown that they have a need (which was the old approach but led to little commitment and follow through) and being helped to appreciate and articulate their wants. A parallel might be drawn with asking 'What do you think of British foreign policy in the Middle East?', which will usually get the answer 'Nothing'; but the question 'What do you think the Government ought to do about X' elicits a positive and even informed response. The framing of the question is important. Similarly, line managers have few articulated wants but they can be led into appreciating them. That is the new task of the training and development adviser.

You may now say that guided self-discovery is little different from the prescription of needs and, properly done, the results are not far apart. The difference lies in the manner of getting there which, in the new method, gains the commitment of the manager concerned. He may not ask for precisely what you feel he needs but, if he can be persuaded to ask for something, albeit cruder and more short term, this is better than accurate prescription which he will resist.

Diary-keeping and self-assessment exercises have already been fully described. The new approach of the training function is to provide such guided self-analysis, to hold a mirror for managers to see themselves in a more objective light and to provide the initial stimulus to make them look. Most line managers are too caught up in day to day problems to analyse the way they tackle their jobs or even the patterns their careers are taking. This fact provides the opportunity for the new trainer to administer a shock, or

85

rather to arrange for managers to administer themselves a shock. Group dynamics exercises, for example, which are enjoyable in themselves and provoke the realization that they could profitably be taken further, have also been mentioned. Once new and important wants have been articulated and managers start asking for help, the rest is easy.

The old abilities

When training was focused on courses, the trainer's skills and abilities were naturally focused on the same place. Lecturing ability with special knowledge of two or three fields was a normal pre-requisite, as were fluent, well-ordered presentations. The old idea of lecturing non-stop for one and a quarter hours and then asking for questions, has been giving way for some time; a lecturer must now have the ability to achieve early and full participation, to introduce humour as well as clarity and to check the understanding of the students.

Some of the best teaching has been done by ex-military or Training Within Industry (TWI) trained instructors. Their ability to break a job down into minute steps, explaining each one clearly and getting the trainee to explain it back makes for good learning; they are aware of the rather slow speeds at which most adults learn and of the wide possibilities of misunderstanding. They have done good work in areas like work study and network analysis; unfortunately their method is not very applicable to the more abstract management subjects and the brighter students resent the slow speed.

Apart from lecturing, many other skills are associated with courses. Attending external courses to vet them for suitability and vetting outside speakers calls for judgement; running one's own course calls for the ability to get agreement on the necessary content and on who should attend.

Administrative abilities have been important. Some training departments grew to a size where simply running them required administrative skill and the Training Boards added to that load. ('Able to understand Training Board requirements' was a phrase that frequently appeared in job advertisments and forecasting grant to two decimal places was an ancilliary skill.) Mounting courses calls for adminitrative skills to deal with arrangements for students and lecturers, cancellations and, with residential courses, the dreaded catering function.

Those functions usually known as management development demand a different range of skills. Agreeing job descriptions, co-ordinating appraisal schemes and preparing succession charts calls for analytical powers and the ability to see what is important. A clear thinking, dispassionate approach is necessary, together with diplomacy, persistence and persuasion in getting line managers to commit themselves on paper.

Salesmanship, which is another word for diplomacy and persistence, has been a quality of all successful trainers. Trainers have had to sell the idea of training, with its intangible benefits, to managers who often had little interest. Analysis of training officers' reasons for attending courses has shown that many were looking for extra arguments to help them to 'sell training upstairs'. Successful trainers have been good at presentation and timing, and the sort of guile which persuades interested senior managers to lecture on their courses so that the others get worried and want to take part.

The burst of post-1964 activity brought a large number of people into training for the first time. Those firms which set up a training department because they had to and were happiest if it kept out of sight, obviously attracted them. Many management trainers were considered as ineffectual and lowly placed, and to have chosen training as a soft option. This produced a self-fulfilling cycle of low expectations leading to low results. Those trainers who were effective used guile and salesmanship and were able to set their sights on the possible and not to worry about the areas where they would never be effective, to seize opportunities for training as and when they came along. (There is a power strike this afternoon, can we do some training?) and to work within the limitations and frustrations of the role. The ability to manoeuvre from a base of nil power was as important as the teaching and administrative skills.

New abilities required

The qualities and abilities required for the new approach to management development are as different as the new relationships and methods imply. The skills concerned with courses are less important and it is a question of assuming authority rather than trying to operate without it. Teaching abilities are still needed, but this is a rather more complex requirement. The act of teaching in the real situation means the tutor has to be able to think on his feet, not necessarily in the sense of providing instant and accurate answers, but he must at least make sensible comment or ask relevant questions. This requires much more courage than being in a classroom where the teacher has prepared his notes and is largely in control of the situation. Many competent lecturers would not risk such an exposed situation and would consider going to teach without every minute prepared as the height of folly.

Part of the necessary confidence and credibility can only come from hard experience as a line manager. To earn respect in a catalytic function, you must see the real problem first and which theories might apply second; you must not appear to be starting with the theories. In one sense the catalytic role is easier in that the tutor does not have to pretend to be the fount of all wisdom; he can admit to not knowing, or to seeing several possibilities and passing the choice back to his pupils. Again, courage and assurance are needed to carry off this role.

The catalyst needs credibility, which is a mixture of experience and confidence, and he needs to be able to get things moving—and keep them going—without doing much of the work himself. He must be able to challenge managers to be self-critical, to answer questions with questions and to watch his pupils making mistakes without

88

leaping to their rescue. His concern is with the learning of his pupils rather than his own satisfactions as a teacher. This is a higher degree of teaching ability and awareness than has so far been practised. It combines the ability to intervene, ie to do the job or effect the change himself if necessary, with the realization that it makes for better learning, most of the time, not to do so.

In the jargon phrase, the catalyst's personal needs must be low. He must be able to subordinate his own ego needs to the learning needs of his pupils; he must also realize that his will not be the glory of the project and his may well not be the gratitude of the project team. If he catalyses successfully, he will be open to the accusation that he has done nothing. In the early stages, even worse will fall on his head as his role induces several frustrations which are likely to be expressed in attacks on him:

he is responsible for managers discovering that they are not managing as well as they had supposed

in the next stage he is seen as having solutions to offer which he is witholding for some mischievous reason

the group is likely to coalesce for the first time in expressing its resentment of him

senior managers are likely to feel threatened either by projects or by the success of the people on the project team, and will express this by attacking the tutor.

The role is not for the thin-skinned or those needing constant applause and approval. The tutor needs a firm conviction of the rightness of what he is doing and needs to know where his loyalites lie. His responsibility is to the organization and not to the individuals although, in prudence, he must ensure that he tells somebody at the top what he is doing.

The catalyst must make his choice of initial exercises in a way that will achieve both action and success. Judging how to introduce the diary-keeping exercise, for example, requires some of the guile and timing already practised by trainers, but steering the early projects into areas where they will produce results requires more of a consultant's 'feel'. Once under way, project teams will provide their own momentum and even terms of reference but initially they need to surprise themselves with their results. Experience in method study or consultancy would be helpful in judging where to steer.

As projects proceed, the tutor may be called on for advice, say on methods of presentation or management techniques (which would be within the competence of the traditional trainer); but he may find himself asking senior managers to allow the project team to have its head, or to be properly critical of the recommendations when presented. This kind of intervention, which is an enabling function, is the stuff of the catalyst's role. He must be able to produce sufficient flexibility in the situation for his pupils to develop themselves and not just run into more articulate frustrations. It follows that he must not be overawed by senior managers and must have sufficient knowledge of their functions not to be deterred by spurious arguments.

There are some specific coaching skills. Apart from relevant experience in depth and the ability to analyse his own experience, he must be a good listener, able to take a convincing interest in other people's problems. As situations arise, he must be able to spot learning possibilities and decide whether it is better to make suggestions, to question his pupil to make sure he has thought out what he is doing, or to do nothing. In the last two cases, he must decide the timing and depth of the post mortem discussion. Third party coaching is different from coaching by a superior: it is more dispassionate but it has neither the authority nor intimate knowledge of the situation. Practice is necessary and is not easily achieved.

T-groups trainers or trainers on the packaged behavioural courses have experience of training a group by leaving them to their own devices for the most part, and intervening only to help the group clarify what they are doing and their underlying motives. Such trainers are also accustomed to being the initial focus of the animosity and frustration of the group; they help the group to learn from its conflicts and not fail because of them. The behavioural trainer's skills can be transferred to management training generally, and so can his sensitivity to personal and interpersonal feelings. It is one of the key tasks of the new management trainer to re-move defensiveness: this can only be done by people who understand the resistances to change and who are experi-enced in getting managers to understand them.

The common factor throughout the discussion of qualities is that of calibre. The new training function needs higher calibre people than have so far been attracted and, in a staff relationship, it is calibre that counts. Senior line managers will take notice of people who are as capable as themselves; they will ignore those who are not. The need therefore is for men who will assume the authority that their function implies; they must have the necessary general management experience and behavioural skill as well as the courage and professionalism that the role demands.

New place in the organization

Developing managers 'for real' implies a new place in the organization.

The training function has traditionally been junior to production, sales and those of finance and has lost any battles it fought against expediency. The function has rarely been consulted before the event in major decisions. Like many aspects of personnel, it has often been given the job of sweeping up after something it ought to have been able to prevent.

As Drucker[1] has said, the succession charts are rarely consulted when it comes to making a sudden appointment, and the implications for the development of managers of such matters as expansion, diversification or re-structuring are considered only after the decision has been taken. The head of management development ought to be in on such decisions, both to contribute and to ensure that he develops managers to meet the company's long term needs. A com-

[1] DRUCKER, P. *The Effective Executive, op cit,* chapter 4.

mon factor in successful in-company development exercises is that they are linked to a major event in the organization. For example, in the early 1960s the Reed Cadre[1] was linked to the need to diversify and to produce more general managers. A major change was taking place and development activities were properly linked with it.

Being able to choose significant projects also implies higher status for the trainer. Occasions like company re-organization form ideal project material; although top managers must take the decisions, they have no monopoly of good ideas. Also, just by raising questions, project teams are likely to clash with some senior manager who would easily find a way of sabotaging them if his rank allowed him to. Trainees often feel (see chapter 6) that they are powerless to change anything, and the trainer may have to assert his authority once or twice to prove that it is worth putting forward proposals.

Training in the real situation encounters far more real opposition than sending people on courses, and the training function has to be that much better placed. It must be represented at court and it must be fireproof in the short term. It is fatal for the new style trainer to appear to be on trial in the early months, or vulnerable to the current month's output figures. All worthwhile changes encounter stormy opposition at the beginning but, once the new approach is seen to be working, everybody will be in favour. The change-agent therefore needs six to twelve months' immunity from the arrows that will be directed at him; thereafter the development function will be accepted as being as important as any other.

[1] See p 21.

11 The right balance of resources

From the range of abilities and experiences called for above, it is apparent that no one man will possess all of them; only the largest firms will be able to employ all the necessary skills on their full time staff. Organizing training in the real situation is therefore a question of assembling the necessary resources, and probably using people who are not officially training staff plus a measure of outside help. Whatever is the right balance of resources, it is important to establish (relatively) permanent and responsible relationships. The case for using part-time or outside help does not mean the occasional use of consultants, with no feeling of permanence or follow through on their part. The correct balance should be worked out to suit the firm's size and sophistication, and the arrangement should be maintained and co-ordinated by one man.

Internal staffing

The ideal team to handle management development would include people with the line management experience and teaching skills necessary for the coaching and catalytic roles. Others should have the behavioural expertise to unfreeze managers in the first instance and to help them to identify and deal with the individual and group conflicts that are bound to arise. The range of skills should thus encompass the traditional skills, plus behavioural and problem solving expertise and general management experience.

The selection of the man to head the function is the most critical step. If he is to be among the five most important

93

men in the firm, and to be listened to at that level, it is likely that he will have made his name and reputation in a senior management job. The managing director should, in theory, be the man with the most all round awareness of the need to develop managers. In a small firm he should attend to the function himself (devoting a fifth of his time to it, not just making occasional noises). In medium sized organizations, the director with responsibility for management development might combine this with other functions but it should still account for one third of his time. In larger concerns, the choice should fall on a man who has not only been successful but has also shown willingness to take real trouble over developing staff, and who can analyse why he manages well.

To my knowledge it has never been done, but responsibility for developing senior managers and their likely successors is a task that could be given to an otherwise non-executive director. The fact that he was part time would not matter if he was supported by a competent man to handle middle managers downwards. The important point is that he would operate at the right level, with a unique blend of authority and impartiality. This seems the ideal way to give management development the status it needs (the idea of giving non-executive directors something to do also has its appeal).

The development function should then provide a coalition of a wider range of talents than hitherto, which will be a strength if they are well co-ordinated. Regular use might well be made of line managers and of people who are not career training specialists. One way of bringing management expertise into training would be to treat it as a function through which the more able managers are rotated, instead of a rather specialist field in which people stay for life. Coaching would not be anybody's first or second job, but perhaps the fourth or fifth, and might be held for two to three years. It is preferable to take experienced managers and teach them how to coach than to take people with a background purely in training and try to give them management competence and credibility.

The other sensible step is to establish stable and committed relationships with outsiders to provide those skills that are not available internally and which it would be uneconomic or impractical to recruit.

Organization development consultants

Organization Development (OD) consultants are perhaps the best known form of external assistance and, although they are behavioural scientists (ie industrial psychologists) rather than management trainers, their work has a bearing on management development and on the real situation. Process consultation as already discussed is a team coaching technique practised by OD consultants and makes direct use of their knowledge of individual and group psychology.

They define their function as helping organizations to cope with change and their specialist skill as helping managers to recognize the various stresses that change produces and, by discussing rather than hiding the resulting conflicts, to overcome many of the resistances. This closely parallels training by projects which often leads to conflicts within the teams and opposition outside them. The OD consultant can thus give the teams a vocabulary and an awareness of the sort of emotional factors that might otherwise limit their effectiveness.

Examples of areas in which OD consultants have mainly been used include trying to make an organization participative when its traditions were autocratic, to smooth out the aftermath of a merger, and to allow a firm to handle a large redundancy in a way that was humane and conducive to good morale for those who remained. When a major change that will affect people's emotional susceptibilities is imminent, OD consultants can help.

The OD consultant is a specialist who should, by observation and insight, be able to diagnose the behavioural inconsistences which are reducing effectiveness either in groups, between groups or through hierarchies. Where the accountant will give predictions about financial performance within given parameters, the OD consultant can give predictions about human performance. This is particularly relevant for policy implementation, new plant development and training in the real situation.

Where good managers exercise their intuitive skills and feel things are going wrong, the OD consultant should help them to 'surface' and articulate these feelings. His essential skills lie in his awareness of the human complexity of organization life, his insight into the human factors which are stifling effective performance, and his ability to offer realistic proposals. He would not claim to be a general management practitioner or to teach management but he has a contribution to make. If you have managerial and teaching skills at a high enough level, you could mount your own training programmes with the help of an OD consultant. He would be expecially valuable in overcoming the initial resistances; again, it is worth keeping him in touch because situations change and working groups change, and even the best ones go out of control. The skills of the OD consultant are the least likely to be available internally, and they are the most important in effecting the change to training in the real situation.

External catalysts

Outside help can range from providing the entire management development function for small firms to dealing with any of the specific functions mentioned hitherto, ie coach, project designer on initial unfreezer. Many of these roles are summed up by the phrase 'external catalyst' which was used in the Mant Report.[1] Alistair Mant defined the role as 'pressing on the conscience of the company, over an extended period of time', in order to consolidate individual and institutional learning. The implication was that it is not a question of spelling out what it needed, which is usually well enough recognized, but of making sure that the needs are not continually disregarded because they are inconvenient or uncomfortable. Mant also stressed the ability of managers to learn from each other, so

[1] See note p 4.

one function of the catalyst is to set up situations for this to happen. By definition, the catalyst is not the fount of all wisdom, but he enables things to take place which, although perfectly sensible, would not take place without him. (Bill Reddin's[1] definition of organization development as 'getting people to talk about things they ought to talk about' makes a similar point.) To pursue the chemical definition, the catalyst's role is a seemingly passive one. His function may have been to select a project team that would learn from each other, to steer them into a profitable area or simply, by his presence, to ensure that the whole exercise does not run out of steam (Case Study 5). The emphasis of learning by discovery is on learning and away from performances by the teacher: this accounts for the strange-seeming role of the catalyst.

The catalyst function can be done by an internal agency, if a firm can justify a man of the necessary calibre full time or if someone is seconded from another division. But there is a good case for using an outsider. The usual arguments for using consultants apply, ie impartiality, a fresh view and time. The outsider has particular advantages in this area because, for example, he is likely to get more honest answers to the self-assessment questionnaire: there is always a suspicion that answers given to somebody from head office would end up in the head office computer. Appraisal of potential can be better done in collaboration with an outsider and questions like organization structures or who might report to whom are particularly political. The necessary skills are scarce, and are most likely to be found in the external agencies. Provided he has the protection of a fixed contract, the outsider is fireproof to the required degree.

External agencies which specialize in this work have certain advantages. They can function part time because their calibre is not required full time and because the real development (ie the self development) takes place between their visits; also they can take contracts for a minimum of a year. The need for mind-stretching in the development of

[1] See note p 34.

managers is continuous, the temptation to backslide is continuous and the successes and failures of one year provide the needs for the next. A consultant should live with his results and his students and, with an external catalyst, the relationship is part time but long term. The learning is in-company, and uses the company's own problems and probably the company's own staff as teachers and administrators.

Specific tasks which can be given an outside agency include:

to diagnose company development needs

to provide the initial unfreezing impetus

to coach, especially senior managers on an individual basis

to select and monitor projects

to represent the development function at the top level

to put new life into a management development scheme that is running out of steam

to spot potential

to arrange succession planning and the planning of experience (in smaller firms)

to bring other expertise, eg designing learning situations for backbone managers, designing training courses for high fliers in companies where geographical scatter makes on-site coaching too expensive.

The ideal relationship, is not specific but general and on-going. 'Diagnose and treat and then keep us up to the mark' are the ideal terms of reference for a catalyst. Usually he will build up the required degree of confidence by carrying out some of the tasks listed above; he will not duplicate areas of internal competence but the permanent and free-ranging relationship not only brings in expertise: it is the best insurance against 'incest' (which even large firms need) and provides the top level follow-through which has so far been the greatest omission of training.

12 Conclusion

Can you do anything about it? Can you teach in the real situation as outlined in this book or is this so counter to human nature and established practice as to be completely impracticable? These questions will arise and many will feel that the preconceptions of training are now too strong and that, having been assigned and accepted a certain status, the function will never achieve any important changes in reality. Put at its bluntest, top management will not let go of anything significant and some training officers will not put up a fight.

Training in the real situation is a very different and more hopeful approach, but it is a complete philosophy, to be accepted or not as a whole. It would be possible to use some of the methods, eg projects, without accepting the underlying theory and realizing its implications, but that would only perpetutate the overall ineffectiveness of the function.

The transformation will not be achieved instantaneously; it is not easy and not everybody will be able to make it. But, it is possible, providing there is basic willingness to develop human assets and good enough people are put on the task.

The concept of training in the real situation is not new but it has been the purpose of this book to spell out the implications and difficulties, to suggest some opening shots and when to bring up heavier artillery. The most important implication is that it is a total campaign and not just a series of skirmishes. Given that realization and a total plan, you can train 'for real' and, as line manager or specialist, your effectiveness will be startling.

99

Appendix 1

Case study: definition of training needs by
self assessment

Two exercises to define training needs were carried out for a service organization which is the market leader in its field. It was not felt there were any outstanding needs and the object was to provide interest and stimulation for managers who, in market terms, had things rather easy.

Groups of eight and 12 were selected, the first eight coming from the most adventurous division, and the second 12 being rather more senior and spread across the company. In each case, the first half day was spent with an outside tutor, mainly to point out the difference between this and the more usual approaches to training. Each member was asked to keep a diary for a week (Figure 1) and was given a self-assessment questionnaire (Figure 2) which was used as the basis for individual interviews a few days later. The managers concerned were possibly more intelligent than average, which may or may not account for their enjoyment of the intellectual challenge of the self assessment, but they spent between three and five hours on it. Many were to be seen earnestly typing their innermost thoughts.

The interviews with the tutor revealed a lot about the firm as well as the individual managers; it was surprising that certain suggestions were then made by several managers—suggestions which they had never made to each other and which they feared would be laughed out of court if they did. Some very pure catalysis was therefore possible, and the tutor had only to feed back the suggestions he had received.

Considerable frankness was also a keynote of the self assessment and one woman supervisor answered the question about her greatest achievement in the last 12 months with 'Survival'.

One of the common features to emerge was that much time was spent in committees so the last half day was spent looking at the problems of working in groups, partly to show how groups can be helped to improve and partly to demonstrate the self-teaching method. After a couple of traditional loosening up exercises (ie four letter words and Lego[1]) the groups were asked to decide what were the most important points to come from their diary keeping. One group of four listed 20 lessons they had taken and had a profitable discussion on which ones they could do anything about. The final group exercise was to make a verbal presentation of what should be the next steps in their development.

A more unusual finding was that the firm had an excess of talent. By its nature, it could only employ articulate men even at the junior levels so, with promotion limited at the top, a barrel-shaped organization resulted in some frustration. The large number of committees was a way of using up the excess time available, but the tutor was able to make a positive suggestion that up to six managers be taken off their jobs for two years and given the task of looking for possible diversifications: they could then sell their ideas to the board and set up the new businesses. This was an unusual idea but it was an unusual problem (and taking six away from their jobs would provide bigger challenges for the rest).

The exercises not only diagnosed development needs, and allowed for a detailed report, but considerable unfreezing had taken place and, more important, the feeling of the beginnings of improvement made for a happy and open atmosphere in which the managers were willing and indeed anxious to learn. The time spent by each participant had

[1] Games using Scrabble letters and children's bricks are used in several courses which look at group dynamics.

been two half-days, a two hour interview and the time he needed to complete the self assessment; the whole exercise was over in less than a fortnight, so this was a good example of getting quickly into the action stage.

Appendix 2

**Case study: an extended course with built
in projects**

This book has emphasized that courses should not occupy
the central place in management training they have so far had,
but there are times when there is no alternative to a central
course, for example when a firm's high fliers are scattered
geographically.

Even so, it makes sense to incorporate the principles of
learning theory as far as possible. The best way to do this is
to split the course into modules, spread it over a year if
possible and set projects in between sessions to reinforce the
lessons just put across. The syllabus of one such course,
which was designed for managers about to move into wider
areas of responsibility is shown in Figure 3, but the syllabus
is not as important as the structure. When properly done, the
projects are more valuable than the lectures and nobody can
complete the course and say 'It doesn't apply to me'.

The sort of projects set are, to find out, after the marketing
lecture, if their firm has a marketing policy, to investigate
selection and dismissal procedures after the personnel
lecture and, after the organization structure session, to draw
out their own organization chart:

 as it is published
 as it is in practice
 as it ought to be

The method study projects are done over two months;
during the first month students define three possible subjects
for method study in their own jobs and they work on one of

them during the next month. Surprisingly enough, these projects have produced an average saving of £300 on an annual basis.

Case example

Two such courses were run in tandem by a large engineering firm. A July-August break seemed prudent, so the 12 two-day modules were spread over 14 months. Over 30 managers were originally nominated, but numbers quickly dropped to about 18. The training department took no part in the selection and later wished it had been more prescriptive. Mixing of ranks, which gave the lecturers problems of where to pitch their material, was another mistake in selection which made the senior nominees resentful and wary. It took eight months' lobbying to get the course moved to a hotel nearby, which made for more comfort; and attention wandered less than when the classroom was in the works.

The course started slowly. Feelings that nothing would change were particularly strong and, as the purpose of the course had not been explained, the initial feeling was one of displeasure rather than joy. If the objects had been more carefully spelled out the course would probably never have started, so the answer is not that simple. In retrospect, the faculty were probably too aggressive in the early stages (understanding of books given out for homework reading was tested) but the initial atmosphere would not have been sweet in any case.

Unfortunately, mainly the senior men dropped out, which meant that the experience and level of participation were lower than that designed for the course. To some extent, this was self-compensating in that the remaining participants dictated the level of discussion and some of the more sophisticated concepts had to be omitted. Another mistake was not to chase every absentee immediately to check on his excuse. The difficulty was one of time and the traditional 'helping' image of the training department, but those who attended were resentful that some managers seemed to get away with it.

Eventually, the course got under way. It came to life in the third month, when a method study by two accountants saved £650 by eliminating two manual copying operations. This success, and the resulting enthusiasm, justified the principle of giving quite crude theory and getting managers to do something with it rather than starting with lengthy and academically satisfying instruction. The work study lecturer was horrified at being asked to cover the subject in four and a half hours, but those who did their project properly learned a great deal about method study.

Three production men bit off more than they could chew. Their scheme to change a stores and handling operation had a potential saving of £2,000 pa but, as one of them explained, 'At first we were treating this as a paper exercise, something for a course but then we thought, why not put it in? So then we started to do it for real. Unfortunately, we kept seeing other good things we could do, and we ended up with more than we could handle within the month.' Those were the words of a man in a learning frame of mind.

After some months, there was evidence of a better use of time, not only among people on the course! The entire accounts department kept diaries for a month and this showed up excess staffing. The computer department took up the idea of job enrichment and arranged a day at which each section leader made a presentation about his job to the others. An investigation into stock control lead to the selling off of £9,000 worth of scrap which, because of an accounting convention (of showing always an average value), was not known to exist.

The quantifiable savings were invaluable for the status of the course, but the more important results were in terms of confidence and personal stature. The two computer managers each thought the other had gained in confidence and their boss confirmed this. One man in his mid-40s responded best of all: he developed from a nail-biting technical specialist to a manager who looked and sounded different and was a definite candidate for promotion. The increases in confidence came from making various presentations throughout the course and from the gradual discovery that subjects which had seemed technical and daunting were in fact within their comprehension.

Other benefits came from the real friendships that arose between people who would normally have avoided each other, because of their function: if they dealt with each other at all, it was by telephone on a 'them and us' basis. The accountants enjoyed their production control projects principally because they had never seen the works and they were pleasantly surprised to find that production personnel were human and not just greasy and illiterate cost centres.

In total, considerable benefits arose from the continuity, the projects and the interaction of participants between sessions. There were successes in applying techniques but the greatest improvements were in the intangible areas of self confidence and a wider understanding of other people and other functions. Those who completed the course were, in a real sense, bigger men, which is what management development ought to be about.

Appendix 3

Case study: teaching by projects alone

A pharmaceutical firm gave an external catalyst the opportunity to teach by projects alone. The catalyst paid fortnightly visits for a programme that was completely unstructured in that no syllabus or subjects were decided in advance. The executives chosen were 12 middle managers in the salary range £2,500 to £5,500, who had been appraised as having the potential to go further. The unofficial terms of reference were to see who had general management potential, as expansion by acquisition was being contemplated.

The participants were all successful and articulate, although several had had relatively narrow experience. They came from a wide range of functions including the legal officer, the quality controller and the organization and methods officer, as well as sales managers, brand managers and accountants. Such was the mix that they were bound to learn from each other no matter what happened. Many of the participants had had considerable experience of the more orthodox forms of training and were intellectually willing to accept the unstructured approach.

Even so, there was a subconscious uneasiness because the participants did not have the normal security of a syllabus (half said this concerned them), or the comfort of take-away notes telling them what they had 'learned'. Perhaps more time should have been spent initially in spelling out not only the intellectual case for dispensing with formal lectures but also the emotional implications of having to take the initiative themselves, instead of looking to the tutor for his customary performance—and reassurance.

The programme began with self-assessment, individual interviews, and diaries. The self-assessments were remarkable for the varying depths with which the managers analysed themselves, and three covered 15 sheets or more. One, the angry young man of the party, said that he spent an entire Sunday on the questionnaire, or rather on the question of whether or not to be honest with it . . . and with himself. He decided in favour of virtue and his boss noticed a difference in him within three weeks. 'He seems to have found himself' was the comment and 'although he personally does not seem to think the course has any particular value, he certainly tackled one job with a much greater sense of responsibility than previously.'

Group discussions on the use of time and subsequent individual projects were only partially successful. An open plan office was partly responsible for this lack of success (and questions of status governed who could have a partition, a door, reeded glass and so forth) but again the initial unfreezing had not been adequate. Emotionally, the managers still did not feel this was an area they could improve or, for that matter, control. The initial projects were poorly done and this had to be pointed out.

The next projects, again chosen by the tutor, went better. Participants were paired with someone from a different function, asked to look at various jobs outside the group and to suggest one or two simple control statistics that would be helpful to their incumbents. One participant who had been particularly uncommitted up to that stage suddenly looked interested. 'You mean for real?' he asked with some excitement and he then saw a point to the exercise. He produced a suggestion that, by spending £70 on a slight programming alteration, a regular print-out could be adjusted to give more directly useful information, and the value of teaching by projects was proved.

Most of the bosses of the participants attended this particular presentation, which showed their support and helped to get the projects taken more seriously. The tutor had met the bosses just before this stage and surprised them by the degree to which he had uncovered the psychological strengths and limitations of his students after a total of only four days' contact. There was considerable agreement on the needs of individuals and it was a mistake at that stage not to commit the plans to writing because later there was an untidy discussion of what had been achieved. By the nature of this programme, it was impossible to set objectives beforehand, but they could have been drawn up at this point and would have been useful later to protect the catalyst's Achilles heel: the accusation that he wasn't doing anything.

The generation of projects then went well. One of the projects on control information had highlighted a weakness in passing information between production and production control and this was felt to warrant a further exercise. The team produced an information board with sliding panels: the tutor refrained from pointing out how clumsy it was, but the team simplified it of their own accord and the system was in operation before the next official presentation to senior management.

Another project was suggested by a participant from among his own problems and, as he was known to have a strong wish to raise his stock levels, an accountant and economist were put on his project team to restrain him. He got his way, but only after much hard work; he produced some new concepts for tackling the problem and was able to get what had been a rigid policy opened up for discussion.

The best project was given by one of the bosses and arose from a proposal by a wholesaler to guarantee a 24-hour delivery service to hospitals in return for exclusivity and an extra discount. The beauty of this project, especially for one manager who tended to see everything in black and white terms, was that layer after layer of problem was revealed. At first it looked like a question of subtracting the extra discount from the saving in distribution charges, but many other questions arose. Were the distribution costs believeable? (The distribution manager's figures were checked.)

Was the wholesaler reliable and what was his reputation in the trade? (The team interviewed him and checked with customers). What would be the savings in invoicing and cash collection costs? (The team listed the items but did not have time to cost them). How could the idea be sold to a certain top manager who was known to be against any exclusive arrangements? (Useful discussions took place on presentation and whether to open with the conclusion or lead inexorably up to it). Would extra sales result from the quicker delivery and what extra volume would be required to compensate for the extra discount? No satisfactory answer was possible without fuller market research and the end result was a further investigation. But it had been an excellent project because it made the team look at distribution, accounting and sales projections, and also go outside the firm to see the wholesaler and sound out customers. Most general management decisions have wide implications and the participants discovered just that.

Other benefits arose from having three concurrent projects in that the teams presented to each other at fortnightly intervals and the need to look further, for example, into the distribution costings was shown up by good questioning from the other teams. The legal officer, who maintained until the end that he could not see why he was on the programme, answered questions about his production control board in great detail and proved the keenest dissector of ther people's projects. The classic case of the quietly spoken man being listened to more and more occurred, and the pompous one was told he was pompous by a woman member in a way nobody else could have done.

The generation of projects went well and the presentation of the major projects was developmental for the bosses as well. The distribution and marketing managers should certainly have discussed that particular question long before but, if the definition of OD is getting people to talk about the things they ought to talk about, then organization development was taking place.

The programme met with many problems which were

instructive. The pace of change in the organization at the time was intense (seven of the 12 participants had job changes announced during the period) and awareness that the projects were incomplete produced its own frustration. The catalyst's role was not understood at an emotional level and, while he was feverishly trying to get rid of the initiative, participants complained he was not giving them enough lead. This might indicate that it is too ambitious to plunge straight into catalytic teaching in a firm which has not used any of the behavioural packages and therefore was not used to the non-directive coach. Alternatively, the programme should have begun with a complete week, probably residential, in which the initial unfreezing could have been taken further and the first feelings of success experienced. With only fortnightly meetings, it was three months before the first successes were achieved and that was too slow to provide the right motivation. This was an informative experiment, with instructive successes and failures, and every credit is due to the firm that tried it.

Appendix 4

Case study: coaching of chief executives

The author spent a week coaching Dr J N Carrington, managing director of Interpet-Liquifry of Dorking, a manufacturing firm serving the pet trade with a turnover of about £¼ million. Needless to say, the week did not fall into any of the categories described in chapter 4: Dr Carrington was virtually free of routine meetings, so there was little to observe. On the other hand, there was plenty of time for discussion and, with evening sessions as well, we spent some 53 hours together. Dr Carrington had asked to be brought up to date with management theory but, with the opportunity to relate theories to his actual situation, we achieved rather more than that.

A word on Dr Carrington is appropriate. Some ten years before, as a chemist in a pharmaceutical firm, he had been sent on a year's management course at Edinburgh at which he gained the top marks in the final assessment. Returning to his firm he found, typically, that they had no particular plans for him so he went into his father's business and sold off most of it to finance the expansion of an £11,000 sideline into the current business. Interpet had just moved into a purpose-built factory, and a management team had been assembled so that Dr Carrington was largely free of the day to day running. The time was right for a reappraisal of where the firm was going.

The first day, Monday, was spent in exploring company policy and in ranging over areas which were giving concern. It is relatively easy to define the policy of a firm when one man owns it (defining policy as the fundamental reason for being, moral standards, etc); even so, talking through one or two seeming inconsistencies was instructive. For example, was it right to aim for a non-punitive atmosphere as being best for learning or should lack of entrepreneurial spirit be countered by a system which imposed penalties for missing targets? Is the danger of over-trading a reason for putting a brake on growth? Other specific questions were the function of salesmen when calling on wholesalers, what market information was available and available in potential, bulk discounts, and what sort of questions could usefully be given to the senior management team to discuss.

On Tuesday morning we discussed selection and interviewing, and the ratio of salesmen's commission to basic salary, and we agreed some preliminary key result areas with the office manager. After one and a half days of loose but wide-ranging discussion it was possible to set the aims for the week. These were to establish a corporate plan, showing what growth should be aimed for, and where and when it would be achieved; and to establish job descriptions and key result areas for the three senior managers. Some form of MBO was necessary, together with a tighter definition of who does what and an understanding of what each manager was to be measured by. Many records had been started but not followed through and appraisals and decisions alike were taken on a subjective and discursive basis. MBO had not been something I expected to cover but I found the need.

The Wednesday also had its free ranging discussions, covering purchasing, complaints procedures, advertising etc, but the greater part of the day was spent in joint session with the general manager, whom I already knew as he had completed a year's course with me (syllabus as Figure 3). The relationship between managing director and general manager was critical, both in defining who did what and in helping the managing director to make the difficult withdrawal from day to day operating. The session was productive in that an organization chart was agreed, which

113

changed as well as formalized the existing situation. More important, a remarkably frank interchange took place in which both men discussed their fears and ambitions and how these had inhibited delegation to date. By chance, there had been a good instance that morning of something which both had eagerly set out to do and this provided a relevant talking point. I knew both men well by then and was able to catalyse a discussion in which there were remarks like 'I think you are empire building'; 'If I delegated that much, I would not know what was happening in my own firm; 'You have delegated that before, and then interfered' and 'You read things over my shoulder.' Such suspicions and fears are at the root of the universal delegation problem: what was unusual was the frank discussion and the agreement to meet weekly to exchange information on what the other had done.

The first and only major disagreement between myself and the managing director occurred during the same discussion. I wanted to press the idea of target-setting as a way of keeping the managing director informed while directing the general manager into the important areas. The managing director felt that this would entail too elaborate record-keeping (time from receipt of orders to dispatch, the percentage of complaints due to manufacturer etc) for the size of the firm. Both sides had valid points but I was able to head off the conflict by changing the subject and giving the managing director a booklet on MBO which he read before our evening session. In it he found an example of a measurement and payments system which answered the question of what targets to set the general manager and also how to pay him on the results (a combination of gross profit in absolute terms and controllable expenses as a precentage of turnover). This had the merit of being easily extracted from data supplied by his small computer and yet was not too detailed. I certainly did not have that particular example in mind, and it may have been luck that the book contained something suitable, but the principle of stimulating the client to produce his own solution worked well.

On Thursday we got down to a long range plan; turnover projections for the major product groups were discussed with the general manager and this was taken further in the evening session by considering a current valuation of assets and whether the projected returns would continue to be satisfactory. During the afternoon, some crude calculations were made to show the sort of figures that would be put into the general manager's incentive scheme. Little contribution was needed from me but it was important for the general manager to be in on the discussions and to carry things far enough for both sides to be committed to doing something. The same was true of a short-term budgeting exercise, but we did enough to prove that tighter budgeting —and more specific control—was possible without too much extra work.

I spent the Friday morning with the salesmen and the office manager. With the latter I concentrated on his view of the managing director's delegation problem and with the salesmen I reviewed their role when selling to wholesalers, their journey planning, what they should do when they had free time, what statistics would be useful to them and so forth. In the afternoon a session with the managing director and the general manager produced a surprising number of decisions. This may have been due to the cumulative effect of mutual respect and clarification of thought, or simply fatigue; nevertheless, several quite weighty decisions were taken. One concerned the only grey area that had been left by Wednesday's organization chart, one changed the emphasis of the senior salesman's role; while the vetting of salesmen's expenses and the keeping of marketing statistics were both put under new people. The general manager agreed to have three major administrative systems tidied up within two months and was given certain extra explicit responsibilities. The managing director and the general manager agreed to go through the post together for a fortnight to provide case law on who was to do what.

Much of the week's work was unique because of the size and situation of the firm and, without a uniquely open managing director, it would not have happened at all. What then is relevant to other occasions? One usual difficulty was that client and consultant began with differing expectations, both expecting the other to structure the day. Such conflict of expectation can always be resolved by more discussion in advance—the standard solution—but this could well have taken two whole days and there is much to be said for beginning with a fluid programme and setting a more specific one as soon as possible, in this case mid-day on Tuesday. The client also felt a need for more documentation which is difficult with a 'diagnose and treat' approach, but this could be met by having a range of books and notes covering all the possible subjects.

The week was successful in getting the managing director and the general manager to be open with each other and in getting decisions on various issues which, for one reason or another, had previously been evaded. The clarification of thought probably took place as a result of ranging broadly and lengthily over several issues and coming back to the important ones, and as a result of pertinent supplementary questions.

Given a suitable marriage of competence and personality, the one-to-one coaching relationship cannot fail to be useful. The purpose is self discovery; this can be achieved as long as the coach has time to create the intimacy and to follow through his line of questioning. This week proved the usefulness of discussing things not possible with colleagues or employees, of checking standards with somebody impartial and, even with a particularly analytical managing director, of sorting out objectives and taking them to their logical conclusion. All these are legitimate functions for a catalyst.

Appendix 5

Case study: a catalytic intervention

This example is included partly for its humour value and partly to illustrate the point that there is often a strong need for someone to do nothing.

The incident concerned a project team: Jack and John who were middle managers in production; Frank and Felix who were managers in the financial accounting area; and Graham who ran a separate internal unit. The project concerned the integration of paper work from the raising of purchase requisitions to the payment of suppliers' invoices, and the team was to have its third meeting with me that evening in a hotel where I was on a programme with somebody else.

We were due to meet a 7 pm. The first indication of difficulty came from Graham who called at 3 30 pm to say the meeting was cancelled. Little progress had been made, the accountants had failed to raise the production people on the telephone, so they had decided the previous evening to call the whole thing off. Felix was going to work late, Frank had arranged to do some private auditing and he himself, who was normally the most reliable, had made irrevocable plans. So far, all quite normal.

I rang the works and was eventually able to raise John, who was still intending to come to the meeting. The only problem was that Jack could only attend between 7 and 8 pm and he (John) could not get there before 8.

At 6 o'clock, I received a telephone call from Frank to say that his audit job was not a big one and that he hoped to be along by 8 30. The project team had run into difficulties because they had learned that the finance director had asked a cost accountant (Smythe) to carry out an investigation into the same area so they had wondered whether it might be prudent to cancel the project. Felix had been offended that someone else had been given the investigation and was all for resigning dramatically.

At 7 o'clock, Jack arrived and over a drink said that he knew about the cost accountant's investigation, which in fact had taken place over a year ago and nothing had resulted from it. The accountants had not been able to get hold of himself or John because a £1m contract had been won and they had closeted themselves away to get on with the necessary scheduling. Frank arrived before Jack had to go and was immensely cheered to learn about the timing of Smythe's exercise. 'I am sure Smythe gave me the impression he was still working on it—he must have been trying to put us off' were his comments.

Jack went, John arrived and we adjourned to the restaurant. John had done an impressive flow chart of documentation which raised Frank's morale still further and excited me as it was apparent that considerable savings, in terms of time and control if not money, would be possible. By the end of the soup course Frank went to ring Felix to try to persuade him to come and join us. He came back with the news that Felix had just taken the dog for a walk and, besides, his car was out of action. At the end of the main course, Frank tried again and came back to say that Felix's first words had been ' Not a chance' and, although he had explained about Smythe, his 2p had run out before Felix was converted.

At this point John went to the telephone and within 30 seconds came back to say that he was going to drive and pick up Felix. By coffee therefore three of the project team were assembled, everybody was talking to everybody again and suggestions were flowing as to the form the ultimate recommendations might take.

The discussion kept throwing up the need for still more

fact gathering and, before the team became totally incapable, they had agreed to meet Smythe next morning to find out what facts he had unearthed, had allocated the remaining fact-gathering and arranged to meet the following Sunday afternoon. The project was under way again.

The role of the catalyst during this intervention had been to make one telephone call, to buy (or did I, come to think of it?) a round of drinks and eat a meal. John Nye was present and directed some comments at the motivation of the group. I asked some questions like 'Well, what are you going to do next?' but I deliberately refrained from pointing to the incomplete fact-gathering or from leading the coversation. The difficulties encountered were no more trivial than usual and, quite typically, the catalyst role was to stop things coming to a stop.

ANALYSIS OF DAY

NAME _____

WEEK ENDING _____

	Things not done that should have been done	Things that (A) need not have been done by me or (B) that took longer than they should.	Who wasted my time?	DECISIONS TAKEN	
				(A) Alone	(B) Shared responsibility
MON.					
TUE.					
WED.					
THUR.					
FRI.					

Figure 1

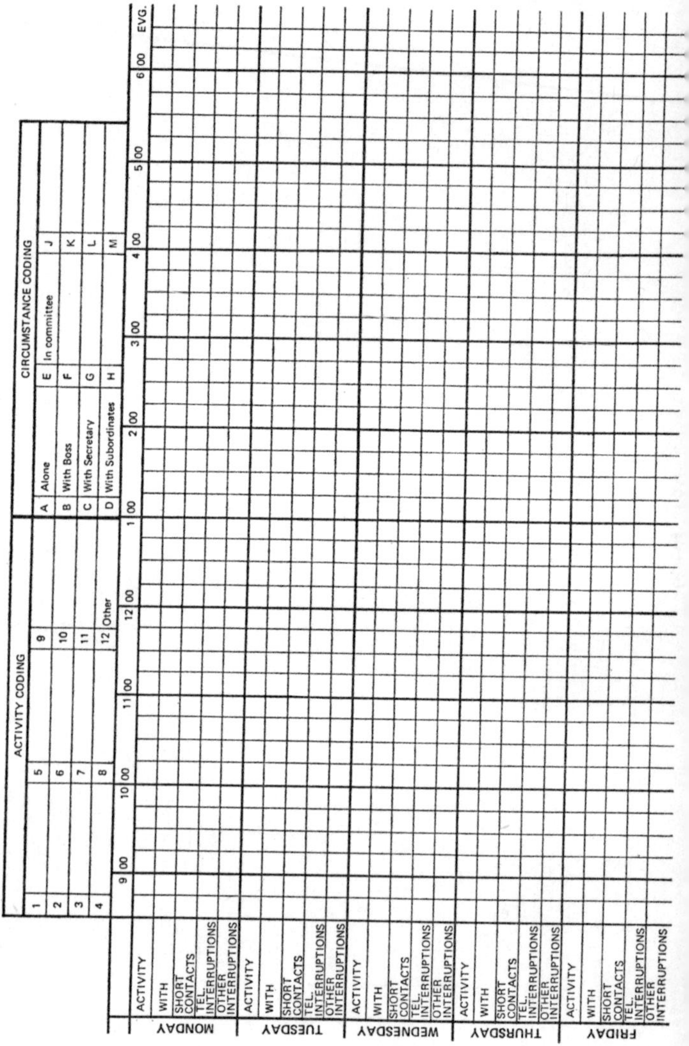

DIARY

Figure 1 (reverse)

SELF ASSESSMENT

Please answer the following questions. There is no pressure to reveal anything you do not wish to, so answers can be long or short, and typed or hand-written. Anything you wish to be kept confidential will remain so. (Put a 'c' beside the appropriate answers).

1. What is your job? It will suffice if you indicate its main purpose, the main people dealt with, and the limits of authority.

2. What are your Key Results Areas? In other words, which are the five or six things which, if done well, will have the most beneficial results for the company?

3. Roughly, how do you think your time is allocated between:
   - (a) Key Result Areas
   - (b) Other Areas, but still necessary
   - (c) Areas of doubtful necessity

   How do you think your time is allocated between:
   - (d) Travelling
   - (e) Being alone
   - (f) Being with one other
   - (g) Being with more than one other

4. What percentage of your time is spent dealing with personnel matters?

5. What would be the typical length of time you get to devote to any one thing?

6. What types of decision do you take, individually and with others, and how often?

7. What are your strong points in the job?

8. What have you accomplished of particular note during the last 12 months?

9. Are there any changes which would enable you to accomplish more during the next 12 months?

10. Is there anything you would like your superior to clarify?

11. Are there any circumstances which frustrate you and make you less effective than you would otherwise be?

12. Have you any skills and aptitudes which are not fully utilised in your present job?

13. What qualifications have you for your present job? Did you get it as part of a wider plan, either of your own or of the company's?

14. Is your present job in line with the sort of career pattern that suits you? Give reasons in either case, and show the pattern you would like to see with an indication of time spans.

15. Would you appreciate the type of career pattern which would give you a change from time to time, even if no promotion was involved?

16. Are there any other points about your work, ambitions or interests which affect the course your career might take?

17. What other (or larger) job could you do?
   - (a) Now?
   - (b) Within a year?
   - (c) Within 5 years?

18. What training and development would you welcome from the point of view of:
   - (a) General interest?
   - (b) Your present job?
   - (c) Possible future jobs?

Figure 2

general management in context

An Introductory Course of 12 2-Day Sessions Linked by Projects & Reading

Session Dates	FIRST DAY	SECOND DAY	PROJECTS
1	**WHAT IS MANAGEMENT?** Planning Operating Controlling **MANAGING TIME** Self Organisation Delegating Priorities	**LEARNING FROM READING** Scanning Active Reading **LEARNING FROM LISTENING** Note-taking Active Listening	Self-Assessment Diary
2	**THE PERSONNEL FUNCTION** Role of Personnel Payment Systems Safety, Welfare etc. **INTERVIEWING & SELECTION** Patterned Interview Responsibility of Interviewer Testing	**GROUP DYNAMICS** Psychological Factors Recognizing Strengths Group 'process' **MANAGEMENT DEVELOPMENT** Tools Available Appraisals Succession Planning	Job Description & Advertisement Organisation of Personnel Function
3	**METHOD STUDY** Observation Techniques Critical Examination Presenting Recommendations **TRAINING TECHNIQUES** Methods of Instruction Aids	**BUSINESS WRITING** Reports Letters Memos	Method Study Report on Theory behind course
4	**BUSINESS MATHEMATICS** Basic Skills Slide Rule Probability Theory **MANAGEMENT BY OBJECTIVES** Job Descriptions Key Results Areas Installing MbO	**TIME STUDY** Direct Studies Synthetics Sampling **NETWORK ANALYSIS** Critical Path Analysis PERT Project Control	Method Study Key Results Areas
5	**PRODUCTION CONTROL** Functions & Types Meeting Delivery Dates Scheduling **STOCK CONTROL** Functions Re-order Levels	**INDUSTRIAL RELATIONS** Principles Trade Unions & Their Procedures "The Bill" **MOTIVATION** People's Needs at Work Motivating & Demoti...	Job Enrichment Production Control

Figure 3

No.			Allocation of Overheads
	BUDGETING Sequence of Budgeting / Control Aspects **COSTING & CONTROLS** Overheads & Allocation / Management by Exception / Set up your own controls	Types of Problem / Fault Analysis / Potential Problems **DECISION MAKING** Systematic Decision Making / Brainstorming	Problem
6			
7	**MAINTENANCE** Planned, Unplanned / Human Aspects / Financial Aspects **QUALITY MANAGEMENT** Inspection & Testing / Statistical Quality Control	**BUSINESS VERBAL COMMUNICATIONS** Presentation to One Man / Presentation to Small Groups / Preparation / Aids	A Presentation Decision
8	**FINANCIAL ACCOUNTING** Provision of Finance / Elements of Accountancy / Balance Sheet Analysis / Ratios	**MARKETING** The Concept / Market Research / Marketing Management **ECONOMIC FRAMEWORK** Applications of Economic Theory / Implications of Economic Factors / Implications of Political Factors	Balance Sheet Analysis Marketing Policy
9	**PURCHASING** Procedures / Price Negotiation **VALUE ANALYSIS** Techniques / Applications	**RUNNING MEETINGS** Chairmanship / Minute-taking **ADVERTISING & P.R.** The Difference / The Techniques	Purchasing Value Analysis
10	**DATA PROCESSING** Hardware / Software / Applications **ORGANISATION & METHODS** Office Systems / Clerical Work Measurement / Office Machines	**ORGANISATION STRUCTURES** Types / Rules / Defined or Flexible? **RESEARCH & DEVELOPMENT** What Sort of Research? / Product Development / Cost Control	Organisation Structure Visit
11	**BUSINESS LAW** Contract Law / Questions Raised by Dismissal / Factory Legislation **DISTRIBUTION** Methods / Transport / Depot Location	**CORPORATE PLANNING** Policy / Strategic Planning / Long Range Planning **SELLING** Sequence of a Presentation / Skills & Personality / Sales Management	Company Policy New Product
12	**BUSINESS GAME** A team exercise to pull together the lessons of the course	**SECRETARIAL PRACTICE** Company Legislation / Role of Secretary **WHAT IS MANAGEMENT?** Final Test / Closing Discussion	Report on Course

Figure 3

IPM Publication

Our current catalogue includes publications of immediate interest to line managers as well as to professional personnel and training managers and students. New titles are added at a rate of one a month.

Members may purchase publications at preferential rates, and generous discounts are available on bulk orders.

If you would like a free copy of our catalogue please write to: Publication Sales Dept, Institute of Personnel Management, 5 Winsley Street, Oxford Circus, London W1N 7AQ.

Some of our publications on training are described overleaf.

Approaches to Supervisory Development
Keith Thurley and Hans Wirdenius

It has been widely realized that general solutions to supervisory questions probably do not exist; what remains is the thorny question of deciding which policy and which approach is most relevant to the situation in hand. This publication is focused on that problem and aims to provide a set of guidelines for management policy decisions by drawing on recent European research studies.

£1; 75p IPM members   92 pp   0 85292 080 6

The Evaluation of Management Training
Matt Whitelaw

The evaluation of management training is beset by problems of definition and measurement. Matt Whitelaw reviews the principal methods of evaluation so far developed to establish what can realistically be achieved at present, and highlights possible future developments in this area.

75p; 60p IPM members   63 pp   0 85292 070 9

Training in Industry and Commerce
E J Singer

This key publication discusses what training is all about, how the training function should be set up, specialist aspects of training, such as management, supervisory, commercial and work force training, training in the small firm and training and change.

75p; 50p IPM members   66 pp   0 85292 002 4

Selecting and Training the Training Officer
Nancy Taylor

A practical guide for those concerned with selecting, training and directing the activities of training officers. Subjects discussed include whether a company need employ a specialist training officer, the role and place of the training officer in the organization, his knowledge and skills, and how to recruit, select, train, develop and use him effectively.

75p; 90 pp   0 85292 066 0